MATTERS OF THE HEART

A Journey of Loss and Encouragement

Janice Petty Wall

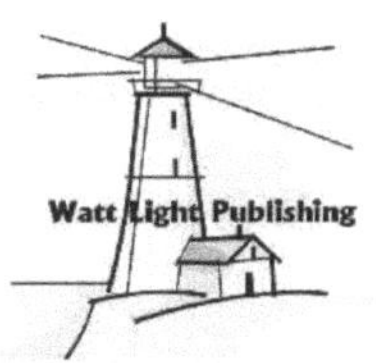

Watt Light Publishing Company
DeQuincy, LA

Matters of the Heart: A Journey of Loss and Encouragement

Author's Email: wall@aeneas.net

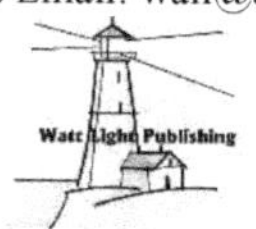

Watt Light Publishing Company
404 LeBlanc Street
DeQuincy, LA 70633

All scripture quotations, unless otherwise indicated, are taken from the New International Version, copyright 1980, Hodder & Stoughton.

Photographs used by permission
The Jackson Book Club: Photo by Rebecca Johnson
G'Pa's Rainbow: Art by Ryan Rehnborg, age 3, photo by Janice Petty Wall
Janice and Parxy: Photo by Lynette Peck
Three Sisters: Photo by Denise Petty Sinisi
The Aguerra Children: Photo by Jessica Gutterez
Needlework of Nativity Scene: Art by Barbara Logan, photo by Janice Petty Wall
Janice and Glenn Wall: Photo by Glenna Wall Waldrep
The Gift of Love: Photo by Janice Petty Wall
Back cover: Janice Petty Wall, photo by Kirby Pines Retirement Community

Library of Congress Control Number: 2020908406

Publisher's Cataloging-in-Publication data
Wall, Janice Petty 1944 -
Matters of the Heart: A Journey of Loss and Encouragement
DeQuincy, LA
Watt Light Publishing Company
124 p.
Includes pictures and illustrations

ISBN-13-978-0-9966807-0-7 Paperback

Subjects: 1. Encouragement -- Religious aspects -- Christianity. 2. Christian life

Summary: The core of this book shares editorial thoughts Janice wrote for a monthly Senior Adult newsletter at White Station Church of Christ in Memphis during 2015-2019. Janice finds humor, comfort, encouragement, and faith in life experiences that we all share. But the heart of this book is her expression of thanks to friends and family who have helped her get through the difficult journey of sadness and loss that Alzheimer's brings. Life must be shared, and it is made easier by friendships along the way.

DEDICATION

This book is dedicated to all the special friends who helped me get through the hardest years of my life—the journey of watching my husband, Glenn, slip away due to his memory loss. All who have gone through this process with a loved one can understand the sadness involved. It is different from the sadness caused by death. It is different from the sadness caused by divorce. It is different.

Like so many life experiences, losing a loved one through the process of Alzheimer's is unique and individual. Yet, without friends to support us, even though they may not totally understand, the process can be impossible to bear.

Life, itself, must be shared. The joys are so much more joyful when there are friends to share. Sorrows and loss are made lighter when there is someone with whom to share.

This book is dedicated to all those who helped me get through these last few years. Some have spent untold numbers of hours just listening, letting me think aloud. Others may not even know of the ways you have lightened the burden. To each of you, thank you. Life was made easier by your friendships along the way.

TABLE OF CONTENTS

INTRODUCTION:
RIGHT NOW IS THE TIME

Right now is the time to get this project completed. Right now the world is in the middle of the Covid-19 pandemic. Oh yes, you remember. You know exactly what is happening in my life, and you can reflect back in your life on those exact days and events, weeks and months. Daily life changed.

It does not matter what you were doing prior to the pandemic, your routine changed. If you had school-age children, you became a home schooler. If you were an emergency room nurse or doctor, your life became more demanding with longer hours and life-threatening contacts. (Of course, that was true if you became a home schooler!) For those in a retirement community which offers multi-level care facilities, life slowed down. No longer is my afternoon spent sitting with Glenn in Job's Way. Early in the spread of the virus in the United States, visitors were no longer allowed in the medical wings. That leaves a huge hole in my day. Several of the activities have been curtailed, leaving more time. I belong to three book clubs, which have discontinued meeting. There is more time.

So now is the perfect time to complete this project that has been rolling around in my mind for several months. Now is the time to get this done. Now is the time to put pencil to paper, words into the computer, which somehow say Thank You to all of you who have been a vital, critical part in my journey for the past few years. Now is the time to tell you what you have meant to me, how you have blessed me, lifted me up, kept me sane, and given me the will and way to continue on.

That may sound dramatic or overstated. However, please believe me when I say in this written way, you will never know the days you kept me from quitting. You lifted me up in small ways and big ways. You provided the strength I needed, knowing you were there with me and you cared for me. Please accept these words for what they are meant to be—giving thanks for getting me through these past few years!

The core of this book contains a portion of the editorials written for the monthly Senior Adult Ministry newsletter at White Station Church of Christ—*Matters of the Heart*. These were written by me during 2015- 2019. This was a hard period of time for me as they were the last "good" years for Glenn.

The journey of losing a spouse or close friend through memory loss is one that is unique to each person who goes through it. However, it is a hard journey, no matter what twists and turns it takes.

Part of the difficulty is that it is so hard to share with others. For me, the difficulty of sharing was that I did not know the words to use. Plus, I felt guilty each time I talked about it, even to those closest to me. I felt like I was betraying a confidence.

Life is so interesting. Each person has their own issues, unique to each one. Yet difficulties are universal. It is a common, shared "problem," "opportunity," "situation" of human life.

MATTERS OF THE HEART:
LEON SANDERSON

Throughout the forty years Leon Sanderson served on the ministerial staff of the Church of Christ at White Station, he filled many roles. By November 2014, when Glenn and I returned to Memphis and to our church home of 20 years prior, one of Leon's responsibilities was leading the Senior Adult Members ministry.

Matters of the Heart was the monthly newsletter designed to communicate activities and give encouragement to the people 60+ years old who attended activities at White Station. This included members of the congregation as well as those from the neighborhood who participated in the many activities offered in the Community Life Center. This newsletter was the brainchild of a couple who worked diligently with the SAM group.

Early in 2015, the couple who had created, written, and produced the monthly *Matters of the Heart* took a job and made plans to move to Mississippi. For some unknown reason, Leon asked me to take over this project. Why Leon thought I would be a fit for this job, I have no idea. I had very little experience with projects like this one. I had not ever considered myself a writer. Why I agreed to taking the job, again I have no idea! However, was there ever a person who could tell Leon "No" when he asked?

Leon had told me that I could commit to trying this job for a few months, then quit if I did not feel comfortable doing this. I think this was as much for Leon as for me. It gave both of us an easy way out if I totally failed!

The project was demanding for me. It would have been simple for someone who had experience with this type of work (or any person 60 years younger than I!). But, it became very important to me. Although many months I would be frustrated with the process, it gave me something to think about other than the decline in Glenn's health. It gave me something to put my mind to other than care giving and medical decisions. It gave me something to think about and produce during the wee hours of the morning when I found myself awake and thinking about "what if, and what next, and how can I," etc. It was one of the many things I can look back on and realize it helped save my sanity.

Thank you, Leon, for giving me the opportunity to serve the White Station church seniors in this way while still being at home where I felt like I needed to be. Thank you for giving me a purpose outside of myself and the situation. Thank you for not giving up on me as I was learning and doing less than a wonderful job. Thank you for being a critical part of this journey over the past years.

The last edition of *Matters of the Heart* was the fall of 2019. The first edition which I worked on was 2015. This "job" certainly filled a desperate need in my life. Leon took a chance on me. I hope in some way it was a blessing to others. But if no one benefited from it other than me, it filled a need that I had at the time.

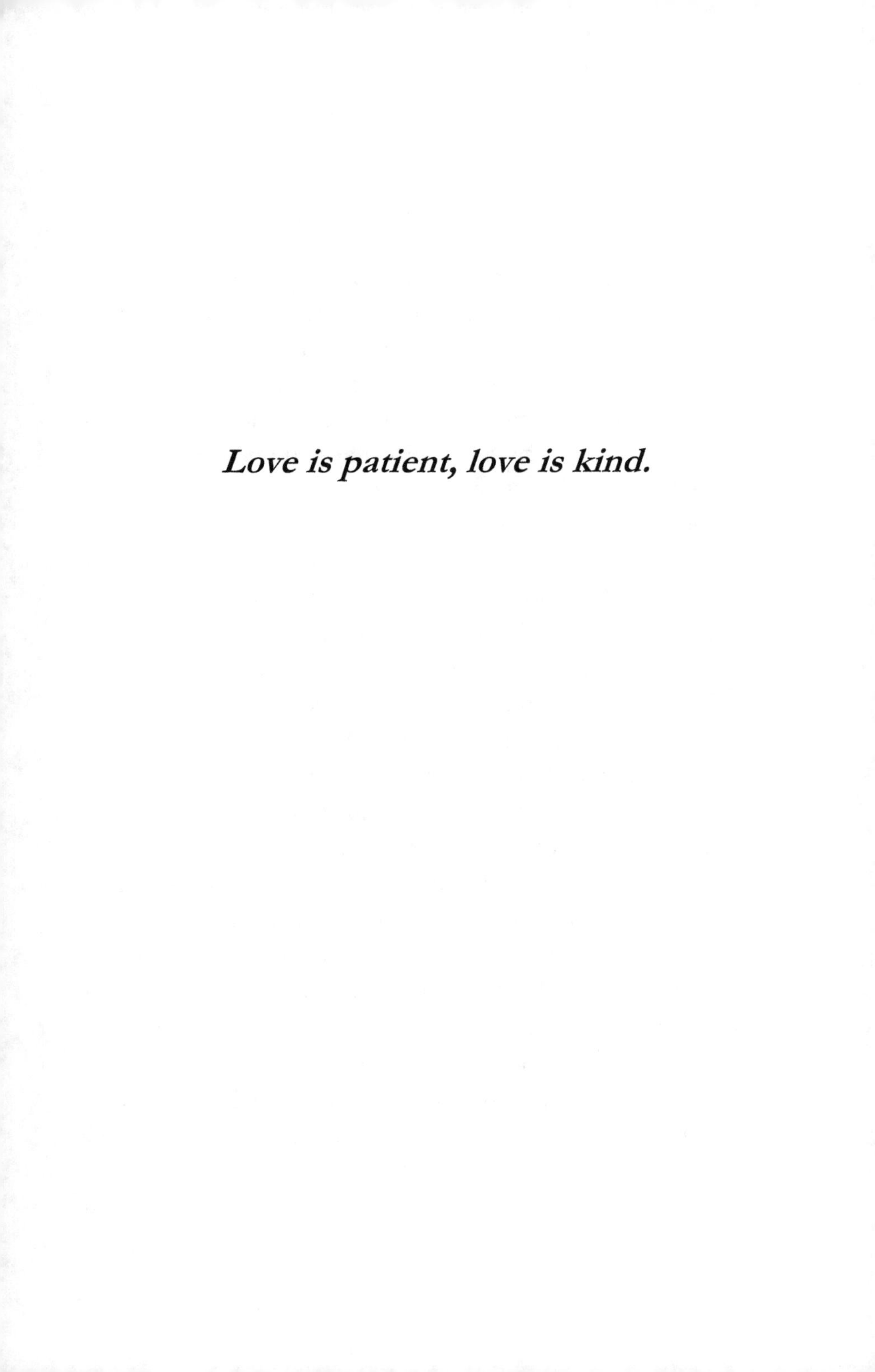

Love is patient, love is kind.

Why Am I HERE?

Oh yes. That same old question asked by so many through the years, centuries, even millenniums. Abraham had to have asked it when things did not seem to be going well after traveling from Ur to his future home. (This is where you called me to come? Really?) And, for sure, Moses must have asked God many times: What am I doing HERE?

As individuals, unless we have been voted into a high political office, or have some powerful court appointment, we really cannot do much about our economy or over-whelming international troubles. However, I can do a great deal to make the lives of those who are also HERE (in my same zip code, in my same community), at this place, and at this time, more pleasant. Last week's title in this same space was "Be an Encourager!" Did I hear a resounding "YES" from the White Station YAHs*?

Yes, I *can* make a big difference in my neighbor's day. I *can* help make a lonesome person feel loved and not quite so alone. I *can* remind someone of the special spot they have filled in the lives of so many. A helping hand with a bag of groceries, a call to check on a person who cannot so easily be out and about, a plate of "extras," a shared book— you fill in the blanks, finish the list, add the ingredients.

You have been placed HERE for a reason. Acts 16 tells of events which landed Paul and Silas in jail. They were probably asking, "Why HERE?" They decided to use their time by holding a singing and prayer meeting. The result was the conversion and baptism of the jailer and his entire family. The answer to "Why HERE" became quite clear.

I and HERE. He has a "work" for me. I only need to open my eyes, listen with my heart attuned, then respond to what He shows me. Mother Teresa is credited for saying, "Not all of us can do great things. But we can do small things with great love." YAHs have a great deal of love to share, and we each can do small things!

*Young At Heart (YAH) was the name of the Senior Adult Ministry at the White Station church.

GIVE ME A BREAK! THANKS, ROY

From the time Glenn and I moved to Kirby Pines, Roy Wentworth has been a huge help. He picked up on the severity of Glenn's memory loss and the demands made on my time and life. Without a thought or any prompting, Roy filled the gap for me. He saw the need and acted upon it.

Kirby Pines has a wonderful movie theater. There is a movie almost every day. Every weekend several movies are shown. Glenn loved the movies. It was something he could do without having the pressure of remembering names or schedules. He wanted to see everything that came our way. The one difficulty with that was he wanted me to be with him all the time.

From the beginning of our stay at Kirby Pines I wanted to take advantage of a variety of activities and opportunities. I enjoyed the offerings in the movie theater, but I wanted to be a part of exercise groups, game groups, and book clubs. I enjoyed walking the trails on the property, especially in the spring and fall seasons. The garden club was an activity that I found fulfilling during the summer months. There were many offerings to pick and choose. I wanted to use time and energy in many of them. There was no way to do it all.

Roy stepped in by coming every week at least once, sometimes twice, to join Glenn at the movie. This was a time Glenn enjoyed very much, having one of his "buds" to share a movie. I enjoyed it because it gave me time to participate in another activity. Sometimes I just enjoyed being by myself.

Roy graciously took this movie time on as one of his many volunteer "jobs." Roy retired in March 2015. Joanne died suddenly April 3, 2015. After Joanne's death, Roy acted as if it were the way he really wanted to spend his time. I know some weeks he needed and could have used the time with some other more pressing job. But Roy was so very faithful in his loving care and time with Glenn. It certainly helped me to have a break each week.

Thank you, Roy, for seeing the need and filling the gap!

*****

Joanne's death came very soon after Glenn and I returned to Memphis, moving into Kirby Pines Retirement Community. The reason for the move was the future we were facing due to Glenn's declining health.

Soon after Joanne's death, I thought perhaps one of the reasons we had made this move at the time we did was to help Roy make the transition. It was not long before my thinking began to change. I realized that perhaps the timing of our move was because Roy truly began helping us make the larger transition in Glenn's life.

ODE TO JOANNE
ONE OF THE GOURMET GROUP
"THE GIRLS"

What!?! No more cream? No more butter?
What are the girls going to do for supper?
We gathered together to share our stories,
Most were happy; some were worries.
We always had lots of fun
Joanne was the funny one.

We became great friends when young.
We were Twenty-six to Thirty-one.
We spent those years happy and single
Teaching and working. Not much time to mingle.
Joanne was sick. We did our parts
Staying up late and sharing our hearts.

Harding was good. Teaching was fine.
On snow days we gathered and had a great time!
Six "girls" stayed together until Death did his part.
Mary was the first of the group to depart.
We shared this sorrow. Life moved on.
Gatherings did not stop, although one was gone.

Life continued along as life will do.
Some lost a parent, then some lost two.
The "girls" stayed single well beyond the norm.
Then things started changing as romance began to warm.
We traveled. We worked. We gathered. We ate.
Then one changed things when she was 38.

Marilyn was the first to take the big step.
Then Joanne and Roy married after they met.
Although husbands were now part of the scene,
The "girls" had their time together, by all means!
There were more marriages as time flew like a flash.
Sadly, death took Marti's husband away too fast.

At some point, the "five" decided we needed
Another person to add class…thus Anita
Became a regular part of the fun,
And even became the special one.
Joanne and Anita were like daughter and mother
They depended so greatly upon one another.

The strong friendship these six "girls" hold so dear
Lets them know love is always near.
As it is in life, nothing stays the same.
Joanne's death suddenly came.
After an evening of a Passover Sader
Joanne was called to go home forever.

Now there are five "girls" to carry on here
This wonderful friendship we all hold dear.
The memory of Joanne will be a part
We each hold dear and deep in our heart.
Thank you, Joanne, for all the laughs
And each special memory of the past.

Joanne King Wentworth
November 11, 1949 - April 3, 2015

by
Janice Petty Wall 2015

Shhh! Sit Still!

Did you know that Psalm 46:10a is the verse most quoted by parents in worship services? Can you remember your parents lovingly quoting it to you about halfway through services? Yep, that's it: The Intentional Parenting version of "Be still, and know that I am God." "Shhh! Sit Still!" Sometimes they quoted the next words: "Pay attention!"

This is not an editorial on child-rearing or proper discipline. It is a reminder to me that God intends for me to sit still and think about His blessings, His power, His creation, and all that He is in my life.

It is so hard for me to really "Be still, and know that I am God." Do you have that trouble? "Be still before the Lord and wait patiently for him; do not fret" (Ps 37:7). What? Be still AND wait patiently for Him? Doesn't He know there are things, good things, Christian things, that need to be done? I don't have time to be still when there is a visit to be made, a call to check on a member, a friend to take to the doctor....

Plus, there is WAIT! No! I am a person of action. I am known for the things I can do, and get done. And "Do Not Fret"? You have to be kidding me! Let's get real about life! But, God **is** real about life. He made us. He knows us, and He knows what we need in order to function properly. He tells us, "They who wait for the Lord shall renew their strength;...they shall walk and not faint" (Is 40:31 NRSV). Also, "Yet the Lord longs to be gracious to you; therefore he will rise up to show you compassion. For the Lord is a God of justice. Blessed are all who wait for him!" (Is 30:1). (There it is again...the WAITing business.)

Maybe this **is** an editorial on child-rearing after all. The LORD is our Father. He is still training us, and will until we take our last breath. I still need to hear Him say, "Be still, and know that I am God."

The psalmist continued to listen to the admonition of his Father in Heaven. "I will sing to the Lord all my life; I will sing praise to my God as long as I live. May my **meditation** be pleasing to him, as I rejoice in the Lord" (Ps 104:33-34). Meditation takes time being still and knowing that He is Lord.

"In the morning, O LORD, You will hear my voice;
In the morning I will order my prayer to You
and eagerly watch" (Ps 5:3 NASB).

Enjoying the Ride? Trusting the Driver?

Forty some years ago, four of us were taking a road trip through the Colorado Rocky Mountains. The beauty around us was amazing. Crossing over yet another pass, looking down into the valley where a picturesque village was nestled, we all agreed it was a storybook scene.

Across the valley, climbing over the next peak, there was a ribbon road, winding its way up and out of the small town. My friend, the fourth passenger, stated very emphatically, "There is NO way I would EVER get on THAT road!" Less than an hour later, we found ourselves on that very road.

The driver, my father, had not said a thing about the plan when the statement had been made regarding "never taking this road." The navigator, my mother, assured us that this was the only road which would take us to our planned destination. The choice was, take this road or get out of the car and find another way home.

Because I had been riding the back roads of Colorado with my dad since childhood, I trusted his driving. Since my mother had never gotten us lost, there was a peace about me, knowing she would not misguide us. I enjoyed the views as we climbed higher, taking the hairpin curves, and reached the summit.

My friend, who had not had the opportunity to trust my dad's driving or my mother's directions, curled up on the floorboard of the back seat and waited for the tumble over the edge of the road, which she felt certain was to be coming at any moment. (The chances of that happening were actually maximized since my dad was laughing so hard tears were running down his cheeks.)

My father was not intentionally causing distress to anyone. My mother was not misguiding us. They had the plan and the road map, and they both knew how to get us where we were to go.

Isn't this how life is? Our heavenly Father knows where He is leading us. Sometimes the road is frightening, but He knows the plan. Jesus lived and showed us how to get to that destination. He gave His all to ensure that we would be able to get back on track when we lost sight of the plan. In addition, the Comforter gives peace and encouragement as we take the roads and follow the plan.

Are you enjoying being this far along in your journey? You know you can trust your Father who is driving because you have been riding with Him for such a long time. He has never led you onto the wrong road. It might have been frightening at times, but He knew where He was taking you. Jesus has been the navigator, giving you clear directions as you go along. And the Comforter has given you encouragement and peace as you have been obedient in following and trusting that all will be well.

Isn't the view from here great? Haven't you seen so much more by going with the Father? Hasn't your life been filled with joy, peace, wonderful surprises, and beauty because you have been on the roads your Father has taken you? Aren't you glad you did not get out of the car and go another way?

JACKSON BOOK CLUB

Since 2010 a very special group of ladies has been meeting as a book club. We meet together each January and select the titles of eleven books we will read and discuss that year. Each has opportunity for input and selection. Subject matters vary. Some books we love, some cause a wide range of interest, and at least one we all said, "Why did we choose that?!"

The one thing we all agree on is that the time with the members of the group is important to each of us. We have been through life's joyful moments as well as sadness and devastation together. Three of the original members have been lost to death. Some have lost parents, some a spouse, some siblings to death since we began meeting. Each has gone through challenging health issues, grandchild angst, life's ups and downs.

Through all of life's joys, sadness, and those points in between, we have had each other. Obviously, many more things are discussed at our meetings than the books. We have discussed, advised, supported, carried each other through life. Everyone needs a "book club." Thanks for letting me be a part of such a special group of ladies.

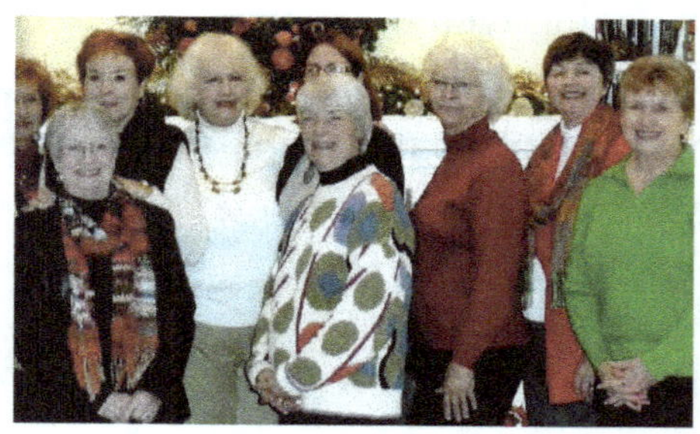

The Jackson Book Club

THE BOOK BAGGERS
SHARING BOOKS, MAKING FRIENDS

Soon after moving, I was asking at the dinner table about a book club here at Kirby Pines. A wonderful lady, Colleen Thompson, said there was not a group, but she would love to help me start one. Thus the birth of The Book Baggers.

The first meeting was January 2015. There were a handful of people, eager to read and share time together discussing good books. That day we established three rules, unlike any book group I have ever known: Don't have to read the book, Don't have to buy the book, and Don't have to give a book report. This sounded like a great group to me!

The Book Baggers group and activities have been such a blessing to me these past five years. The time spent on planning and organizing the activities, writing a monthly newsletter for communication, and getting books for members to read has been very fulfilling and joyful for me. In this time of confusion and uncertainty with Glenn's declining memory, my energy and thoughts directed to something I could "control" gave me some peace. The book group has been affirming and supportive. The members are appreciative and express thanks for the time and effort.

Thank you, fellow readers and book enthusiasts, for the fun times you have provided, for the kindnesses you have shown, and for your interest in this activity. You are a group of people who have no idea how much you have contributed to my well-being during this time.

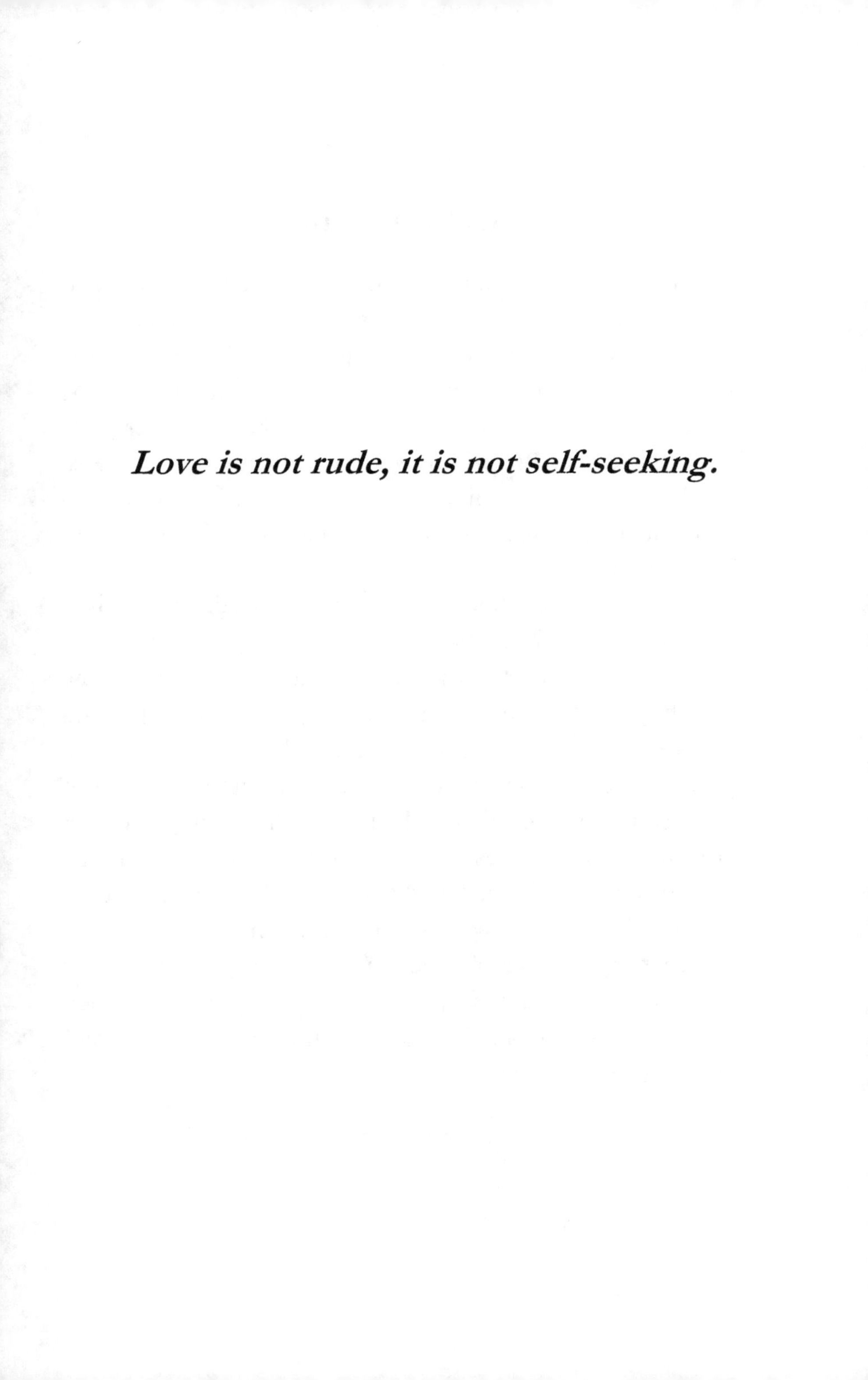

Love is not rude, it is not self-seeking.

Welcome 2016!

Another new year with new beginnings, determination to improve, to keep those promises we have been making to ourselves and others. (You fill in the blanks.) Good for you if you are a person who makes New Year's Resolutions. At least you have given some thought to what a "better you" might look like. We all know we will break most of those resolutions at some point. At least we have looked at ourselves again and recognized opportunities for improvement in our daily living.

Here is a resolution that is probably worth considering. Romans 15:13: "May the God of hope fill you with all joy and peace as you trust in Him, so that you may overflow with hope by the power of the Holy Spirit." Paul is praying for the Roman Christians to be filled "with all joy and peace." These Christians were being persecuted because of their belief and obedience. Paul was challenging them to "trust in Him." The result of their trusting in God would be an overflowing of hope "by the power of the Holy Spirit."

Think about life with a proper trust in God. What else do we need than God, Jesus, and the Holy Spirit in our lives? Paul emphasizes the need for trusting in God when writing to the Roman Christians. In this 15th chapter, Paul quotes from scriptures:

Rejoice, O Gentiles, with His people (Deut 32:43 NKJV).

Praise the Lord, all you Gentiles!
Laud Him, all you peoples (Ps 117:1 NKJV).

This is the God I plan to trust in 2016—the One who asks me to rejoice, praise, and sing. If He can "rule over the nations," I will trust Him—praising and singing, being filled with joy and peace. (And yes, I will probably add the resolution of losing some weight during 2016. Why should this year be any different?)

March: Something for Everyone, Joy for All

March has something for everyone. For basketball fans, there is March Madness. For all who claim to be, or want to be, or have friends who are Irish, there is St. Patrick's Day. For those of us in a hurry to get the day started, we have Daylight Savings Time. We will turn our clocks forward so we will get up earlier and stay up later. (Or just get tired earlier.)

How about something for those who like to do scientific experiments? March 20, the first day of spring, Vernal Equinox, or Spring Equinox, is the only day of the year you can balance an egg on end. Did you know that? It's true. I've tried it. (How is that for useless information?)

Tuesday, March 1, will be "Super Tuesday." This is for everyone who is watching the once-every-four-years event in our country of selecting a presidential candidate to represent each party. (Some would say this is also useless information.)

Each of the above-mentioned days and events will be of great interest to some. Others will not even notice. However, there is one day in March that is extremely important to everyone. March 27 is Easter.

Forgiveness   Completeness   *Freedom*
Adoption into God's Family   **JOY!**

Easter, the day to celebrate and remember the resurrection which took place 2000 years ago. It causes us to be thoughtful as well as joyous. That resurrection morning changed the history of the world. It changed our future for eternity.

Easter is for everyone. The resurrection of Jesus, the Perfect Lamb of God, is the reason for joy, hope, and peace.

Easter is the one event that truly is for everyone!

Enjoying the Beauty while Trusting God

The month of June is already here! Spring has come and gone. Soon the heat of summer will be in full force. Flowers have popped up, and trees have gotten their summer leaves. There is beauty all around us as the winter and spring are already forgotten.

There are challenges with this time of the year. There is wind and usually rain. Tornadoes and other storms have already begun to show their force while the northern hemisphere tilts toward the sun. These storms can be powerful intrusions upon many lives.

One of the advantages we have by living to our ages is that we know these storms will come and go, just as they have all our lives. They are a part of the life we live. The awe of nature, new life, and the beauty around us far outweigh the storms which come with the change of seasons. Let's exercise our **Trusting** resolution through any storms that come our way.

This time of year may bring new energy and a new outlook on each day. It does for me. If I could sing, I would be singing at the top of my voice. If I could dance, I would be twirling, skipping, and leaping. (I do that in private once in a while. It is a dangerous activity and **not** a thing of beauty to behold!)

Most of us have aches and pains. Storms come into our lives periodically. However, we have God to reassure us that we are free, forgiven, and safe, and we are His children. Let us live in awe of the beautiful world. We just might go ahead and sing as if no one is listening and dance like no one is watching! (I will do it if you will. Try not to break anything.)

Sing to the Lord, you saints of His; praise his holy name.
For his anger lasts only a moment, but his favor lasts a lifetime;
weeping may remain for a night,
but rejoicing comes in the morning (Ps 30:4).

You turned my mourning into dancing;
you removed my sackcloth and clothed me with joy,
that my heart may sing to you and not be silent.
O Lord my God, I will give you thanks forever (Ps 30:11).

WEDNESDAY EVENING
SUPPORT GROUP? BIBLE STUDY? FRIENDS!

From my youngest years, I remember going to the church building on Wednesday evening. Some of the places we lived referred to this time as "midweek services." Other places, it was simply referred to as Bible Study. Glenn grew up calling it "Meeting" night. Whatever we called it, Wednesday evening was a marker for the middle of the week. Our weeks were marked by worship on Sunday and "Bible Study" or whatever on Wednesday. I wondered how others kept their place in time without these events. Very few of my weeks prior to turning 70 years old did not have these events.

Then came the move to Kirby Pines Retirement Community, November of 2014. I was 70 years old when we moved. Glenn was 82. It was a time of new patterns in our lives—New living situation. New friends. New everything.

Although Glenn and I returned to our previous home church in Memphis without giving it a thought, we made the decision it was time to consider our "old" age and make some changes. One major change was not getting out much at night. That meant no "midweek services." Sure enough, I found that my weeks felt disjointed. I had trouble placing a "midweek" marker. Plus, I missed the fellowship of a ladies' group, which all the Bible-study groups had been for me for the last twenty years.

About the same time Glenn and I moved to Kirby Pines, a neighbor from Jackson also made the move. We knew each of us was making plans to make Kirby Pines our home at some time in the future. However, Glenn and I had no idea Iris would be moving within a few weeks. Iris was now a widow. She had fallen and broken her back. Her plans quickly included the medical wing at Kirby Pines for several weeks.

Iris knew no one except Glenn and me at Kirby Pines. Although I knew many residents from my previous years in Memphis, they were all acquaintances. So Iris and I began our own "midweek services," "Bible Study" or whatever. We began with just the two of us. Very soon, we included another lady whose husband was dealing with similar issues as Glenn. Then a neighbor of the newly added lady became a member of the group. And thus began our permanent midweek ladies' group. There are now seven of us who meet. Although we have no formal name, we know what we are: a very important support group.

Some might think this is a gossip group, but we make a conscious effort not to be that. We talk about many issues. We keep up with what is going on in the lives of each lady. Each one of us feels free to share concerns about ourselves and our family, believing these confidences are kept just within the group. There is much laughing. Most of the weeks are very uplifting and positive. Once in a rare while, we slip into some negative conversations. But we make the effort to steer away from the dark side. We do stay away from politics and rarely lean toward the negative.

Thank you, dear friends, for filling a special need in my life. Not only have you provided emotional support during this difficult time, you keep me in touch with what time of the week it is!

G'Pa's Rainbow

Why is it that we keep all those pictures the kids, grandkids, and now, perhaps, the great-grandchildren have drawn, pasted, finger painted, painted, etc., for us?

When we were making our recent down-sizing move, everything I touched had to have a decision made about it. *Throw away, give away, or take to the new place.* Many things that had seemed so special at one time ended up in the "throw away" pile. Other things of great value to me were given away (forced upon some unsuspecting relative or friend). However, about half of our 4' x 6' "attic" space is filled with boxes of those masterpieces by the little ones.

Why are these of such great value? It caused me to think. It is amazing how down-sizing can cause us to truly re-align our thinking.

The value of these artistic gems lies in the love I have for the one who created these "priceless" pieces. I *love* these little humans who put that effort into their work. I remember the occasion they presented that work of art to me. One of these beautiful pictures, "G'Pa's Rainbow," is hanging on a wall in our very small, *limited wall-space* apartment.

As grandparents, you don't need to be told the reason. You have them also. We love the ones who created these modern-day "Picassos." God, our Heavenly Father, is the creator of each of us—all of us. How well we realize that we are not perfect. How greatly is that reality shown to us every day. This world is filled with imperfect, not-so-beautiful humans. However, our perfect Father created each one of us. Just as we love the results of those small fingers who presented to us a precious, not-so-beautiful piece of art, shouldn't we love the "human" works of art our Creator placed on this earth?

I may not understand each person I meet every day. These people may not look like me. All of us don't think the same way. We all have different points of view, different history, different background. However, each of us is a child of our Father, the One we love, praise, trust, and worship. Just as I love Him, I must love and appreciate His creations. Let's determine from this day on we will do our best loving each other because God created us, and He said, "This is very good!" Part of loving the Creator is loving His creation.

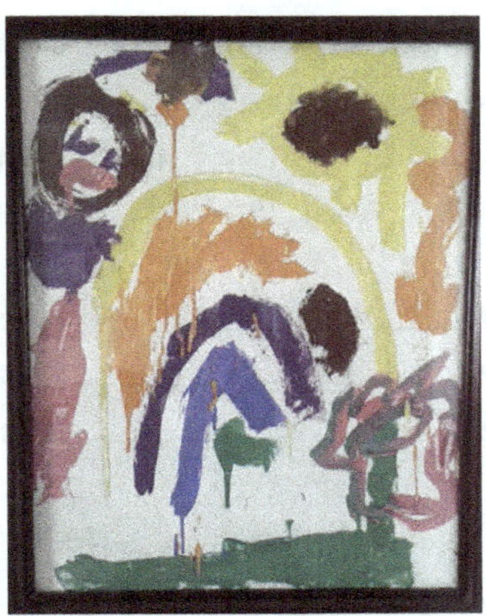

G'Pa's Rainbow
Art by Ryan Rehnborg, age 3

Safe Home Base

A favorite childhood game in my neighborhood was "tag." Undoubtedly you remember that game well. It was a favorite any time a group of children had an outdoor activity and time on their hands. No equipment was required. Very few rules applied. And any number of children of any age could play.

"Tag" began by one child volunteering (or being elected) to be "it." "It" would chase the others, touch another child, shout "you're it," passing the responsibility of chasing others to the new "it." You remember.

The one nice "rule" of the game (in my neighborhood anyway) was there was always an object or space called "safe," "base," or "home." This could be anything—a tree to touch, a large rock to climb onto, or a sturdy adult who was willing to stand in one place and be grabbed. When the chasees (not really a word, but you get the picture) touched the designated "safe," "base," or "home," the current "it" could not turn over the chasing duties/privileges.

There were no winners, no losers. The object of the game was to have fun. The end of the game was when the participants ran out of energy. Or, in my neighborhood, the end came when one of the mothers called "dinner time" and all the neighborhood kids dispersed to their homes for an evening with their family.

As an adult, do you feel like you are participating in a version of "grown-up tag"? Many of you YAH members (60 years old +) are in the peak of your careers. You have more responsibilities now than ever before at work. Many of you have added duties with volunteer work. You are the age when our congregation expects a great deal of you for your wisdom, advice, and talents.

This generation is called the "sandwich" generation for good reason. Some of you are caring for grandchildren periodically or permanently. Others of you are now caring for a parent who is in need of part-time or full-time attention. There are some of you who are called upon to take care of grandchildren as well as parents at the same time.

Those of us who are a part of the "fully retired" group probably are still feeling torn between what you are able to do and the things you feel you should still be able to do. You have been active all your life doing for others. Now you are still wanting to do for others, yet your strength and abilities are slipping away. You can no longer do those many "good works" you know need to be done.

As an adult, do you have a "safe" place? Is there a "base" place you go to feel totally grounded? Is there a friend you have who makes you feel secure? When you enter your place of living, do you feel at peace?

The word "home" invokes different images to each of us. However, could the word "heaven" invoke that sense of the perfect "home"? As long as we are upon this earth, we need those places of "time out" just to rest and relax. We all are running toward that ultimate "safe," "base," "home." The longer I am here, the more I look forward to heaven, my home.

THE MAHJONG GROUP
SUPPORT GROUPS OF ALL TYPES

Support groups come in all shapes, sizes, and types. There is a group of ladies which meet on Monday and Friday afternoon each week, sometimes more often, to play mahjong. These ladies make up a support group that meets emotional needs in all seasons of our lives, at any level to which we rise or fall, in occasions planned and unplanned.

On the last Monday of July 2019, the day of Glenn's move to Job's Way, these ladies provided the best support anyone could have provided to our family as we went through the physical effort and emotional strain of making that hard step of physically separating Glenn's and my living areas.

Mary Ann* had asked if they could provide lunch for us. The kids, who were here to make the move, and I had decided we would not take a lunch break all together. We would get lunch in the Bistro or dining room as we felt the need. Each of them had eaten breakfast at different times. Some of them had brought some food. All of us were on a different eating schedule and diet. One on Keto diet, one on Noom, one on high protein and grains (all very healthy diets), and I on anything that met the emotions of the moment (Unhealthy!). So, of course, I told Mary Ann not to bother. We would be fine, had a plan,—etc.

Sometime late in the morning, I came to the apartment to get something. Spread out on the table was the most beautifully presented gathering of healthy, appetizing food I had seen in a long time. There were finger sandwiches, fruit of all kinds, cheese and crackers, nuts, and even some chocolate (dark, healthy, of course). There were pitchers of ice-cold fruit tea, plain tea, and water. There was a large platter of raw vegetables and dips. There were cold cuts of meat and a variety of breads.

I cannot begin to remember all the bounty that was provided. I do remember the sight and the emotion of love, caring, and being wrapped in a big hug from the mahjong group who were somewhere in the building, thinking about Glenn, me, and the family as we went through this time that we needed basics such as nourishment of food. Beyond that, we needed the love and caring that they were providing in their quiet, gracious way.

Of course, the kids all came to the apartment, and we took a break together. During that time of eating, we shared our thoughts and feelings. We rested physically and shared emotionally. It was time we needed together to express our feelings and thoughts. The hour and a half that we spent together was far more restful, healing, and helpful than any of us realized we needed or would ever have.

Thank you, members of a "ladies' game group." The real purpose of the group is to support, feed, honor, and meet the needs each member has. Oh yes, we enjoy playing mahjong. But that is not half the story!

You each mean more to me than I can express. I would say you mean more to me than you know, but I think most of you understand it. Otherwise, you would not have gone to the trouble to make that meal happen!

*Mary Ann and Roy Thurmond live down the hall from me. Both have been such a great blessing. Mary Ann was the coordinator for the food provided on moving day, and Roy was the mover of the all-important recliner. They have been a critical part in my adjustment to living daily life without Glenn.

Christmas: God Wrapped in Flesh

How will you wrap the gifts you are giving this Christmas? My sister-in-law is an artist. Her gifts are always a work of art. Not necessarily the gift itself—I am talking about the way she wraps the gift. She will have a cut-out of a wintery scene. Or, she may have a miniature Christmas tree blinking with little lights on the package. Sometimes she will paint the wrapping paper herself. Yes, it is a magical array of beauty under the tree after she has carefully wrapped and placed each gift, enticing us to enjoy the gift even before knowing what the actual gift might be.

As for me, I am a real fan of gift bags! It has been years since there has been any gift "wrapping" done in my house. The person who came up with gift bags is a **real** inventor. In my opinion, that person ranks up there with Thomas Edison and his light bulbs, Johannes Gutenberg for his printing press to produce the Bible and all kinds of books, and George de Mestral who invented Velcro! (Look that one up for yourself.)

The most unique and best wrapping of all time has to be the Real Gift sent to the stable that wonderful night so many years ago. God came to us wrapped in flesh. Just think of how unique and practical that was.

The Godhead knew that we humans needed a way to learn what God looked like and how He wanted us to behave. For centuries, humans had been making their own images of "god." So God the Father sent God the Son to earth wrapped in flesh, looking like a baby, a real human infant! Who would have thought? (Our Almighty God, of course.)

Just think of how practical that wrapping was. We humans can relate to flesh. We understand flesh. (At least we thought we did until this special Gift came along.) This baby was loved from the beginning. This present lived a life just like the rest of us do. The wrapping stretched and changed. Our Gift experienced growing up with all the joys, sorrows, and surprises the rest of us experience. As our needs change, this Gift changes, yet really stays the same.

The wrapping was used year after year until it had served its purpose and was no longer needed. Then the wrapping was discarded, and the Gift went home.

What a wonderful Gift we received wrapped in flesh. He is waiting for us to join Him in that permanent home when it is our time to discard our wrapping.

There Is a Savior
There is a Savior, What joys express!
His eyes are mercy, His Word is rest;
For each tomorrow, For yesterday,
There is a Savior Who lights our way.

(Lyrics by Greg Nelson, Bob Farrell, and Sandi Patti, 1986)

*Love is not easily angered,
it keeps no record of wrongs.*

2017: What Resolutions Will I Make?
(And Break?)

The January 2016 *Matters of the Heart* challenged us to live life trusting our Father by the power of the Holy Spirit, with encouragement to be filled with joy and peace, spending time rejoicing, praising, and singing. How did you do with the 2016 challenge? January 2017 brings us another opportunity to look at ourselves and the way we are living, examining corners of our lives that need to be dusted, polished, and adjusted.

Knowing that the resolutions made for a new year are generally broken before the year is a month old, one year I resolved to eat what I wanted to eat and exercise only when I wanted to exercise. My thinking was that there would be a year in my life when resolutions would be kept. It worked. However, my life was not improved in the least.

What would a "better you" look like? What would you be willing to spend a year focusing on to improve the way you think, live, treat others, and deepen your walk with God? Perhaps this "better you" can help form resolutions that would be worthy of keeping for a year.

Some of my New Year's Resolutions for 2017 will be:
* Start each day with prayer, Bible study, and meditation.
* Treat each person I meet with respect and kindness.
* Control my tongue (such a difficult one!)
* Be patient with those closest to me (even more difficult).
* Be more relaxed.
* Lose 10 lbs.

Are these generic enough? This list looks much like the

list I make most years. Do you think it will be possible to keep these resolutions all 365 days of 2017? Not likely. But I will be a better me if there is an effort to live this list each day. You can help me by pointing to the error of my ways when you see me slipping. (Except the one about the lbs.!)

February: The Month of Love

Have you ever been responsible for writing editorial thoughts for February, the month of "Love"? You might think that would be the easiest month of all.

There has been so much written about love. Everyone loves love. We all have experienced love. There are so many wonderful poems about love. And, of course, there are so many scriptures about love.

Therein lies the problem! What does one say about love that has not been said? What can be put on paper that is wise, thoughtful, fresh, and new about the subject? If you have some words on this topic, please volunteer to write this column next year.

As for me and this year, I am sticking to the best that has been written. You will get nothing new from me! Hopefully, these scriptures will serve as reminders of the true essence of love.

And he passed in front of Moses, proclaiming,
"The Lord, the Lord, the compassionate and gracious God,
slow to anger, abounding in love and faithfulness,
maintaining love to thousands, and forgiving wickedness,
rebellion and sin" (Ex 34:6-7).

Do not seek revenge or bear a grudge against one of your people,
but love your neighbor as yourself. I am the Lord (Lev 19:18).

May your unfailing love be with us, O Lord,
even as we put our hope in you (Ps 33:22).

Your love, Lord, reaches to the heavens,
your faithfulness to the skies (Ps 36:5).

There are many verses telling about love. This would be a great month to search the scriptures about God's love.

The Devil in the Morning

Each morning as I settle into my time to be alone with God, it seems as though an uninvited guest comes along.

The routine is to settle down in my favorite spot, with just the right light, sometimes with a cup of freshly-made coffee, and open my Bible to my beginning place. Proverbs will get my mind focused on the words of wisdom God has for me today. Perfect!

The problem this morning, as is true so many mornings, is the devil is up early to join me. You would think as busy as the devil is at night, he would not be awake and working at 4:30 a.m.! When does he sleep?

It seems that no matter what time I settle into my special place, that ancient character can find his way into my space and my mind. How does he do this? One morning it might be the unfinished tasks from yesterday which catch my attention. Another morning it is an event in the future which is on the calendar that grabs my thoughts. This morning it is the schedule of today that comes creeping into my mind and will not go away.

Do you experience anything similar to this? Does the devil come into your time with God? What do you do? Whatever it takes, I must take control and send the devil on his way! This time alone with God is too important to let that sneaky little character deter me.

If you have any secrets for success, feel free to pass them along. I can use all the help you can give!

In the morning, O Lord, you hear my voice;
in the morning I lay my requests before you
and wait expectantly (Ps 5:3).

Be still, and know that I am God;
I will be exalted among the nations,
I will be exalted in the earth (Ps 46:10).

I will sing of your strength, in the morning
I will sing of your love; for you are my fortress,
my refuge in times of trouble (Ps 59:16).

I cry to you for help, O Lord;
in the morning my prayer comes before you (Ps 88:13).

I rise before dawn and cry for help;
I have put my hope in your word (Ps 119:147).

I wait for the Lord, my soul waits,
and in his word do I hope (Ps 130:5).

How precious to me are your thoughts, God!
How vast is the sum of them!
Were I to count them, they would outnumber the grains of sand—
when I awake, I am still with you (Ps 139:17).

Let the morning bring me word of your unfailing love,
for I have put my trust in you.
Show me the way I should go,
for to you I entrust my life (Ps 143:8).

And one final perfect example:

Very early in the morning, while it was still dark,
Jesus got up, left the house and went off
to a solitary place, where he prayed (Mk 1:35).

I'm guessing the devil did not join Jesus on this occasion. He might have tried, but Jesus knew how to keep him away. Jesus had run him off before.

Beauty and Usefulness

Recently, my sisters, sister-in-law, and I met in Hot Springs, Arkansas, for a week of visiting, laughing, and "whatever." On one of the "whatever" days, we decided we would spend the day outside of town experiencing a zip line, digging for gems, and touring a crystal mine. This tour included information about the formation, the grading, and the uses of crystals, which make them valued and useful.

As is true of many things of beauty, a crystal is formed by many years of extreme pressure and heat. The greater the pressure and heat, the clearer the crystal becomes. The most valuable crystals are perfectly clear, multifaceted, with smooth sides and sharp edges.

Crystals have been admired and appreciated for their beauty for many years. However, it was not until 1880 that a use was discovered beyond the sheer enjoyment of their beauty. As you probably know, the first use was the development of the "wireless" (radios). Today we all benefit from crystals in electronics, computers, cell phones, and highly developed machines used for scientific and medical purposes.

In order for the gem to be used for electronic purposes, the beautiful crystal has to once again be put under extreme pressure and ground into small pieces. The beauty has to be sacrificed for the new purpose. The crystal has to be re-formed, "squashed or stretched" as described in one article I read.

Is this what God has in mind for our lives? Haven't we been told that we will be tested by fire? Do we sometimes have to allow ourselves to be crushed and reformed into something more useful? We must die to ourselves to become the perfection of what God has in mind for us.

After the day of digging in the dirt, the best "gem" I found was the reminder that lives of beauty and usefulness come about by God's shaping, testing, and molding.

Each of us 70+ grannies came away with some zip-line stories that we hope will impress the grandkids and make our children shake their heads and question our sanity. (Why not keep them guessing?)

SISTERS/SISTER-IN-LAW
TRIP TO HOT SPRINGS

March 2017, a "Sisters/Sister-in-law" trip was planned. It turned into a wonderful trip with four of us. We enjoyed the famous Hot Springs baths with the full spa treatment—very relaxing. We shopped, ate, played games, and laughed.

One day was spent searching for diamonds and riding the zip line. Kay, our sister-in-law, spent most of her day on the zip line. It turns out that she was the most adventurous one of the four of us. Her grandkids would have been impressed.

The times spent with the "girls" through these past few years have been so special. Laughter is easily initiated with this group. Nothing special is planned. We take each day as it comes. It is a joy to relax with each other. Since we do not live near each other, it is easy to miss out on day-to-day news about family events. We catch up on news from each family.

In addition to time we have spent together on any trip, my sisters and sister-in-law have each come to Memphis and spent time with me here at Kirby Pines since Glenn has been transferred to Job's Way, the memory-care wing. Each trip and time with these special people in my life has been an encouragement to me. The time together since Glenn's move has been especially uplifting.

Thank you for taking the time to be with me, here in Memphis and other trips of adventure. Each time we are together, you are an encouragement to me.

THE WORLD-WIDE TOUR OF
COFFEE HOUSES IN THE MEMPHIS AREA

November 2014 was our move to Kirby Pines Retirement Community. The decision was made by both of us. But Glenn was the final driving force for selecting the location as well as the timing. Glenn knew what he was facing if he continued to live. Kirby Pines has a wonderful memory-care facility. That was the selling factor.

In addition to the retirement community and medical facilities, Memphis is where many of our dearest, long-term friends lived. It meant I was returning to the home town of most of the members of my "Gourmet Girls" group. Of the six original "girls" in the group, four of us were now in Memphis. (Marilyn, Sally, Joanne, and I were here. Marti lived in Henderson. Mary had passed away years ago.)

It was nice being back where these friends from our single years could get together easily. Marilyn, Sally, and Joanne were at Kirby Pines the day the furniture came. (Glenn was still in Jackson finishing up things from that end.) They came in and directed the placement of the furniture, helped get my kitchen sorted, and made the bed. What a blessing! I was at a loss, and they knew just what to do.

Unfortunately, just five months later, on April 3, 2015, Joanne died suddenly. This was a shock to everyone. The evening before, we had been at a Passover meal at the church building. Roy called early Friday morning to say that Joanne had died during the night. His world had been suddenly turned upside down. The "gourmet girls" had a big hole in their world.

One of the things Joanne and Roy loved to do was visit all the coffee shops in Memphis. Checking out the new trendy coffee shops in Memphis had been their main Saturday outing for some time. Joanne kept the rest of us informed of the new coffee shop trend in Memphis.

In honor of Joanne, Sally began researching the coffee shops and began planning what we soon dubbed as "The World-Wide Tour of Coffee Houses in the Memphis Area." The three of us who lived in Memphis now frequented a different coffee shop weekly if we could. It became our time together. It is where world problems were hashed and rehashed. It is the time we shared our lives. It was my "therapy" time.

There is nothing like friends who have known us through the many seasons of our lives! These are the friends who share our hard times without having to talk about our hard times. These are the ones who know what we are going through without having to dwell on it. These times together were my "pressure valve" to keep the pressure cooker from exploding.

During this time, we shared the death of Sally's mother. We shared Sally's terrible schedule of continuing to hold a job, yet going to Little Rock, Arkansas, every other weekend to spend time with her parents—and now just her dad—because she is the girl in the family of four siblings and the one who lives the closest. Sally is no longer holding a job, but now is spending more time in Little Rock trying to meet the needs of her "independent" dad.

Hopefully the times the three of us have together while we continue our WWTCHMA are as helpful to Sally as they are to me.

Thank you, Sally, for planning our WWTCHMA!

*****

WWTCHMA times are just the beginning of Sally's role in my "sanity" these past few years. Although Sally has not been mentioned by name in several of the other episodes told in these "Thanks" notes, she has been a part of many. Sally was a late stay and early morning return to the hospital visit mentioned elsewhere. She has been a part of transportation with other doctors' appointments and procedures. Sally has been available at just the right time and place.

Right now, during the "stay at home" limitations during the Covid-19 days, Sally hosts our WWTCHMA times via Zoom conferencing. Each week, Marilyn, Sally, and I set up our "coffee house" in our own homes for our weekly visit. Now, that is a game-changer!

A Powerful Funeral

The service was held at 10 a.m. on Monday. We were there to remember the life of a 91-year-old lady* who had been semi homebound for several months. Her name is not found on any list of "the rich and famous," "greatest accomplishments," or "Guinness Book of World Records." Normally there would not be many people in attendance. However, additional chairs had to be brought in to this large chapel to accommodate those who had come to honor and remember this lady. She obviously was not an "ordinary" person.

What made this lady so special? Her obituary looked like so many others we have seen. "She was born to…on…in…." "She was preceded in death by… She is survived by…." "She was a devout Christian and an active member of…." However, there is one line in the middle of the details which I have never seen in any other obituary. This line explains a lot: "She was known for her love for babies."

This one fact defined and directed so much of her life. It molded her attitude and actions with everyone she touched. Her life's work was with babies who needed love and families who needed help. What started as a volunteer job became a critical piece to the healing process of babies and families at a large children's hospital. When she was not caring for babies and families who were hurting, this precious lady was encouraging and helping others who crossed her path. This 91-year-old had spent her life loving people from their birth to death.

After the meal for the family and friends, we expressed final condolences and sympathy to her husband of over 70 years. He smiled and said, "I know I will be grieving later. But right now, all I feel is happiness! We made it!"

A powerful funeral is a great reminder that my obituary is being written right now. What will that obituary say? Will it be as simple and as powerful as "she was known for her love for babies"?

*This wonderful lady was Sally Cook's mother. Sally is one of the Gourmet Girls and the organizer of WWTCHMA.

Help Wanted!

"Help Wanted" signs are sometimes posted in windows of stores needing to add staff members. There are "Help Wanted" ads found in the Classified Advertisement section of newspapers. Companies let it be known when they are needing help.

Generally, we travelers on this terra firma are not so public about our needs. We don't put a "Help Wanted" sign out for others to see. There are some "Help Wanted" signs for humans for which we should be on the alert.

Help Wanted!
Apply Within

A heart may be breaking because of situations out of our control: the loss of a loved one, a rebellious child or grandchild, loss of a job or financial support, severe illness—this list goes on.

Help is needed from a friend. This help is needed for the heart and mind. Loving deeds and words are required. Balm for the heart and mind must be applied. This balm comes from an understanding friend, from a stranger who does a kindness unexpectedly, words from our Father. Whatever the form of help needed, it must be applied to the heart and mind. It must be applied "within."

Help Wanted!
Send Email

The internet seems to be the most common means of filling out forms, finding and providing information, and transfer of requests and information. Fortunately, when we are having a "Help Wanted" issue, we have one main address that works: Dear God! This address works every time. It works for additional times. When we are especially thankful for life, "Dear God!" is a good way to send that message. When we have a deep emotion needing to be shared, "Oh Father" is a good place to start. "My Comforter" is a good address for sending anxieties and concerns. They all get your message to the right department.

Help Wanted?
Read Instructions

These words often arrive in a box full of unassembled parts. We might have ordered a wanted piece of equipment or furniture. What arrives at our doorstep are nicely packaged bits and pieces which include everything we need to put together our wanted item. To successfully end up with our desired item, we really need to read the instructions and follow them step by step.

My mode of operation generally is to begin assembly and then read the instructions when I run into a problem. This is not the best way to approach a box full of bits and pieces. Nor is it the way to approach life! (Why do we learn this lesson so well only after we have tried and failed so many times?)

MARILYN

How does a person express appreciation for someone who literally keeps you going? Marilyn was that person for me during most of 2018-2019. Marilyn seemed to call at just the time I needed to hear a voice of reason. Marilyn was the one I could count on spending a couple of hours a week with talking about anything and everything. She let me talk about nothing important, or something important. She would understand if I wanted to talk about "the journey of sorrow" or did not want to even come close to the subject. She was the one to whom I felt comfortable enough to say anything. She did not judge, or misunderstand, or offer a suggestion. She somehow instinctively understood that I did not want suggestions or sympathy. I just needed to have a sounding board.

Marilyn was the one who set a weekly coffee time for the two of us to meet and talk. This was a big sacrifice for her since she had a time schedule that was full. She was the one who was called on to do so much for so many. But she carved out a minimum of two hours a week for me during the months that I needed it the most.

I can never express enough how much that time meant to me. Some weeks I thought there was no way I could make it. But the "time out" with Marilyn kept me going. She always had a way of taking my mind off the situation or focus on it—whichever was needed that week.

"Drinking from the Saucer"
by John Paul Moore

I've never made a fortune,
And I'll never make one now
But it really doesn't matter
'Cause I'm happy anyhow
As I go along my journey
I'm reaping better than I've sowed
I'm drinking from the saucer
'Cause my cup has overflowed
I don't have a lot of riches,
And sometimes the going's tough
I thank God for the blessings
That His mercy has bestowed
I'm drinking from the saucer
'Cause my cup has overflowed
He gives me strength and courage
When the way grows steep and rough
I'll not ask for other blessings for
I'm already blessed enough
May we never be too busy
To help bear another's load
Then we'll all be drinking from the saucer
When our cups have overflowed.

This poem is a reminder of God's word which tells us of His steadfast love.

The steadfast love of the Lord never ceases,
His mercies never come to an end;
they are new every morning; great is your faithfulness.
"The Lord is my portion," says my soul,
"Therefore I will hope in Him" (Lam 3:22-24 ESV).

The Head of Your Parade

Recently, while visiting a lady in a health-care facility, I asked how she kept such an upbeat spirit and peaceful outlook on life. She answered quickly and very confidently without hesitation.

Her answer? During her late teen years, she had hitched her wagon to Jesus. He was the head of her parade. He had never led her down the wrong path or through a dangerous alley. She was absolutely sure He would lead her the rest of the way!

This totally confident, ready answer caused me to ponder. The way she said these words were not just a saying she had heard sometime and considered it to be a cute answer. It was a conviction she had lived by for many years. It was the guiding light of her life. It is what she had kept in mind each step of the way.

At some point in the conversation, this kind, sweet lady asked me who was the head of my parade. She was asking me where I found my moral compass. Where do I turn for guidance?

These are questions well worth pondering. No matter how many years one has lived, it is good to spend time rechecking our motivating influences periodically. With life sending conflicting messages of all kinds through news, entertainment, reading material, companions, pressures, it is a good exercise for me to check my moral compass periodically and look to see who is leading my parade.

So let me ask you: Who is the Head of your parade? To Whom do you look to be your North Star? Have you hitched your wagon to Jesus and stayed securely with Him?

Our adult classes are currently studying John's gospel. John tells us: "These are written so that you may come to believe that Jesus is the Messiah, the Son of God, and that through believing you may have life in his name" (Jn 20:31 NRSV). Is Jesus the Head of your parade of life? He will never lead you down the wrong path.

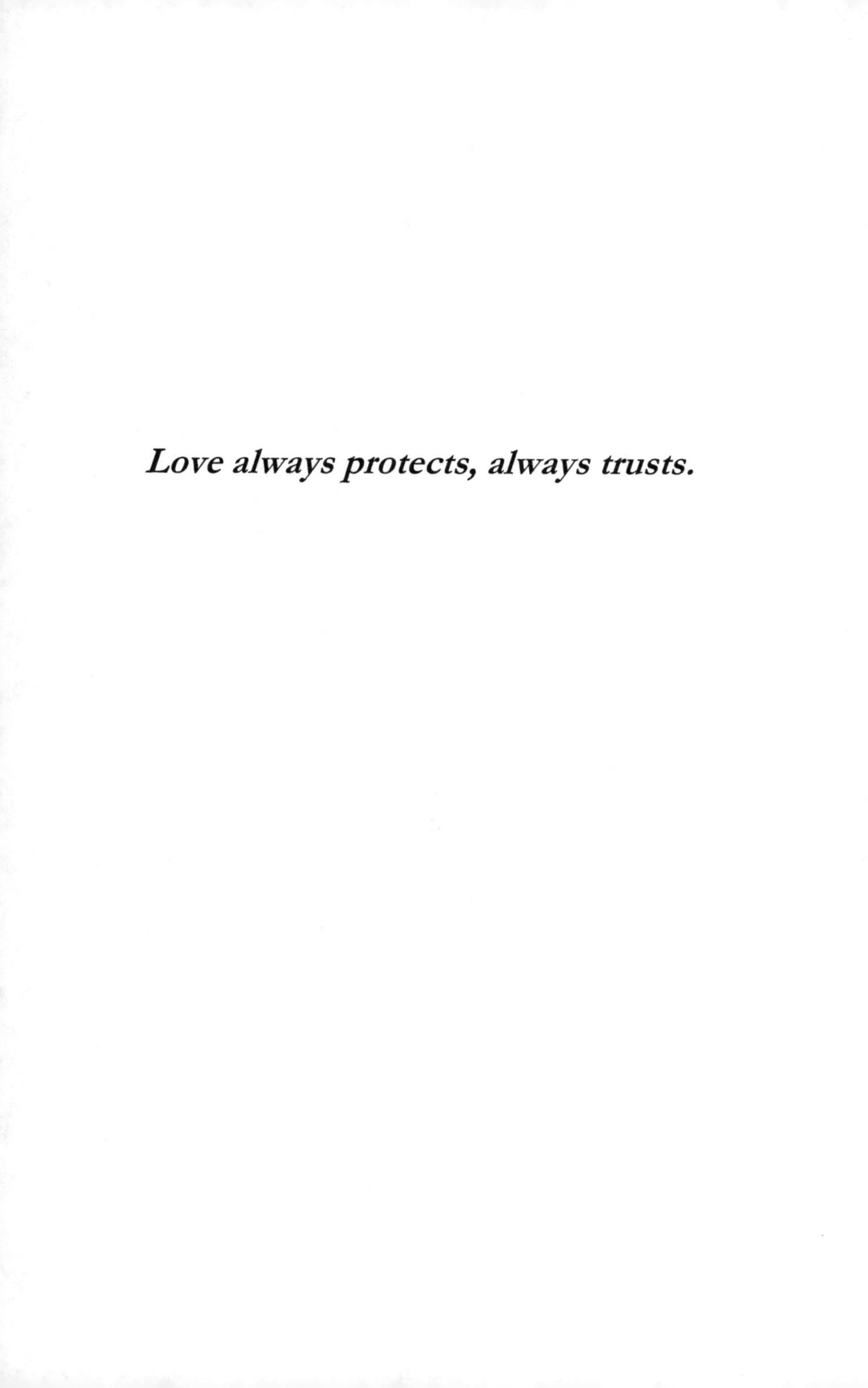

Love always protects, always trusts.

Taking Inventory

The first job I had with an actual paycheck lasted five days. I walked to work and home from work. The hours were 6:30 p.m. until 8:30 p.m. For these two hours, a large number of "lucky" high school girls counted. It was the annual inventory for a local ladies' clothing shop. We touched every item in the store. The colors were noted. The sizes were checked. Each piece of sparkling costume jewelry was itemized.

By the end of the week, the manager knew exactly what had been sold, what needed to be moved, and what gaps needed to be filled. They had taken inventory! Every business has a method of self-evaluation. They take inventory. With computers, most retailers have an ongoing update with every sale. (Not nearly as exciting as it was in the "olden" days!)

Self-evaluation is generally a healthy thing to do. Quick daily checks are good. However, a thoughtful annual check this time of the year can be helpful, productive, and challenging.

In this space of our monthly *Matters of the Heart* the past two years, there have been suggestions/challenges for individual self-improvement. The 2016 challenge to us was to be more trusting of our Heavenly Father. The intended result was a life of joy and peace. The 2017 article encouraged us to spend the year "focusing on ways to think, live, treat others, and deepen your walk with God" in order to be a "better you." My personal list for 2017 was:

*   Start each day with prayer, study, and meditation.

*   Treat others with respect and kindness.

*   Control my tongue.

*   Be patient.

*   Be relaxed.

*   Lose 10 lbs.

How did I do? As you would imagine, some days were better than others. (Of course, I still have those 10 lbs. to work with!)

It is inventory time. I am determined to "note the colors, check the sizes, and itemize the costume jewelry." There will be a new and improved list, making a note of actions and thoughts that need to be adjusted, added, and deleted. This exercise is good. It will encourage me. There is a Manager in charge who is helping me to improve my business of living each day.

Psalms in the Night

What do you do when you wake up in the early hours of the morning and cannot get back to sleep? Do you keep a good book close by to occupy your mind? Do you get up and work on a project that needs to be completed? Do you exercise? Do you eat?

This morning at 3 a.m., I began doing all of the above in reverse order. Coffee and cereal were first on the agenda. (This guarantees no more sleep for the night!) At this moment, my Fitbit says these legs have traveled 2.41 miles. As you read this article, you are seeing the fruits of my labor for this month's project of *Matters of the Heart*. And the good book close by to occupy my mind? The Psalter!

The adult Bible classes at White Station have been studying Psalms this quarter. We began the last Sunday in January and will continue through the last Sunday in March. Don't you just love the psalms? There is something for all seasons of life. Even those short seasons of sleeplessness. Those who wrote the psalms were no different than we. They had nights when they could not sleep. And they took pen in hand and wrote their thoughts, making good use of their darkest hours.

> *Ps 1:2—But his delight is in the law of the Lord, and on his law he meditates day and night (NKJV).*

> *Ps 16:7—I will praise the Lord, who counsels me; even at night my heart instructs me.*

> *Ps 42:8—By day the Lord directs his love, at night his song is with me—a prayer to the God of my life.*

Ps 63:6—On my bed I remember you; I think of you through the watches of the night.

Ps 77:6—I remembered my songs in the night. My heart meditated and my spirit asked.

Ps 119:55—I remember your name in the night, O Lord, and I keep your law (NKVJ).

The next time you are awake when you should be sleeping, read a good book. How about trying the psalms. It can bring some peace. It might even help with sleep.

TENNIS ANYONE?
A FRIENDSHIP FOR A LIFETIME

How does God put just the right people in your life at just the right time? That is a puzzle only God is able to work out. Parxciene (Parxy) Peck Moore is one of those blessings God sent to me at just the right time.

Parxy and I met the first day of arrival on the campus of Oklahoma Christian College. I had "thoughtfully" chosen OCC simply because it was the college my older brothers and sister had NOT chosen. All through high school, I was known as "Charles', Vera Jeanne's, and Jimmy's younger sister." I wanted to be ME.

So there I sat. Alone. Unpacked. Nothing to do as classes had not yet begun. Wondering how I was going to make friends. Then I heard someone yell down the hall, "Parxy, I can't play tennis. I have to…." Without thinking or even sticking my head out the door, I yelled, "I'll play with you." Thus began a college friendship, and that blessing of friendship has lasted a lifetime.

Although Parxy and I have not lived near each other since college days, we have stayed in touch. The past few years, we have tried to meet for a few days at a half-way point in Arkansas. During those days, we laugh, visit, and laugh some more. It always amazes me how easily I laugh when Parxy is around. Even our telephone conversations are half catching up on family news and half laughing about anything and everything.

Parxy has always been medicine for my heart. Especially these past few years, our quick visits on the phone or at our quick getaways in Arkansas, the time together has meant more to me than Parxy can possibly know. She lifts my spirit. She encourages me to keep going.

Thanks, Parxy, for playing tennis with me that first day at OCC when I was so alone. Thanks for being available during these times of needing a good hearty laugh!

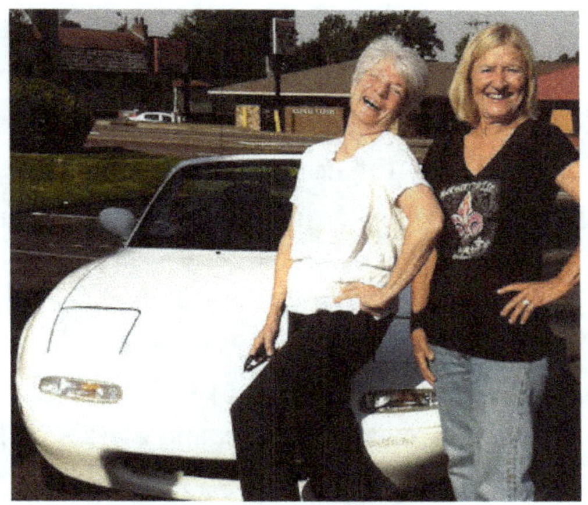

Janice and Parxy

*****

April 29, 2020, Jean Saunders (editor and miracle worker of this book) and I were spending the evening going over the first draft of *Matters of the Heart*. The doorbell rang. It was a package being delivered. The package was a huge box of custom-made cookies sent from Parxy. What a lift to my spirit. Yes, Parxy, you make me laugh! Thanks, as always!

'Til the Storm Passes By

Today I am trying to complete this article for our monthly *Matters of the Heart*. As often happens, I am pushing the deadline. At 2:40 p.m., as I was beginning to put my thoughts on this page, lightning struck a transformer nearby. All electrical power failed. The lights went out, the computer went blank. Of course, my first concern was for all my work. Had it been wiped out? Then I thought of one of my favorite songs:

'Til the Storm Passes By

In the dark of the midnight I have oft hid my face,
While the storm howls above me, and there's no hiding place.
'Mid the crash of the thunder, precious Lord, hear my cry;
Keep me safe 'til the storm passes by.

Many times Satan whispered, "There is no need to try,
For there's no end to sorrow, there's no hope by and by."
But I know Thou art with me, and tomorrow I'll rise
Where the storms never darken the skies.

When the long night has ended and the storms come no more,
Let me stand in Thy presence on that bright peaceful shore.
In that land where the tempest never comes,
Lord, may I Dwell with Thee when the storm passes by.

'Til the storm passes over, 'Til the thunder sounds no more,
'Til the clouds roll forever from the sky,
Hold me fast; let me stand in the hollow of Thy hand.
Keep me safe 'til the storm passes by.

(Lyrics and music by Mosie Lister, 1958)

The storm did not destroy my work on the computer. However, it did remind me of the beautiful power of a storm and the peace that can be experienced by remembering that God is with me through all of life's storms—no matter what the form or nature of that storm. The next few minutes, I spent listening to several musicians on Pandora singing their versions of "'Til the Storm Passes By." What a soothing time that was.

Don't you love to have powerful moments when you are assured of the peace you have because you are God's child and He is in control? This song has reminded thousands of the peace in God's strength and love. No matter what your storm, may you experience God's peace through that troublesome time.

JANET REEVES: HELPER, ORGANIZER, RESIDENT MEDICAL ADVOCATE

Janet and her husband, Gerald, moved into Kirby Pines a couple of years after Glenn and I had moved here. We had known them from church many years, but more from a distance.

As soon as they moved here, Janet became very involved in many of the activities I had been enjoying while here. She joined The Book Baggers group and soon became very active in helping with the details of the monthly meetings. Janet is one of the members of a smaller group of readers that a few of us ladies enjoy. Janet learned to play mahjong and soon became a regular at "our" table. She is a member of the mahjong group mentioned elsewhere in this collection of ramblings.

Janet was the brains behind our monthly "Girls' Night Out at the Movies." She saw a need for a "ladies only" activity and got busy putting that into place. Janet provides the popcorn each month. We usually have a close to full house for this event.

Janet's career had been in the medical field. She had worked with doctors in hospitals for many years. She understands how they work, and she knows what patients need. She also seems to know how to talk to doctors. I learned this first-hand a few months after Janet moved here. I was scheduled to have a very minor surgery which generally was an outpatient procedure. By this time, Janet knew something of Glenn's condition. I had expressed some concern about returning home after the procedure. My concern was not for the success of the procedure, but the responsibilities I would face at home.

At the time of this procedure, Glenn was still able to get to the dining room for food. He was still able to get himself to bed and dressed in the morning. However, when I was home, Glenn wanted me to cook for him and do more for him than I thought I might feel comfortable doing within a few hours of the procedure.

The surgery was scheduled for early in the morning. Janet got me to the hospital. Marilyn and Sally met us there. The three of us spent most of the day in that "holding" space. As oftentimes happens, the surgery was delayed until mid-afternoon. I was still in recovery until early evening.

Being a former medical person, Janet was allowed to be with me in recovery. She was with me when the doctor, a rather tall, muscular man, came into the recovery room and said I was being dismissed to return home. Janet, all 5'1" of her, stood up practically toe-to-toe and told him **"NO!"** He would not dismiss me to return home! He would keep me overnight!

I was still foggy, but I do remember being amazed that Janet would have the nerve to do that. I was even more amazed when the doctor did not question her, ask her to explain, or even give a hint of arguing with her. He simply changed the orders. I was quickly made very comfortable in a private room for the night.

Thanks, Janet, for understanding what I needed and being my advocate. I still don't know how you pulled that off. But it surely was nice to have you there to make those arrangements.

Before We Were Yours

Lisa Wingate is the author of a New York Times best-selling novel, *Before We Were Yours*. The fictional story is inspired by events which took place in Memphis at an orphanage operated by Georgia Tann. Many children were snatched from their homes or taken from their mothers at birth and sold to families in California, New York, and many locations in between.

Recently, Ms. Wingate was in Memphis, making several appearances to tell the story. She also had arranged for a "reunion" of people who had been adopted from the Tennessee Children's Home Society. Several of us had the privilege to attend one of the events and hear stories told by some of the adoptees. Although it has been almost 70 years since the last child was adopted from Georgia Tann, the raw emotions still pour out as these people tell their stories.

One gentleman's words continued to haunt me through the day and night. He had been told that his mother had willingly given him up. However, he could not believe this could be the truth. He stated, "She gave me a name. Why would she have named me if she planned to give me away?" This man knew that his mother had loved him. He still feels it in his heart.

Isn't that the way it is for us? Not only are most of us blessed to know the love of our earthly parents. We also know the love of our Heavenly Father. Ecclesiastes 3:11 tells us: "He has made everything beautiful in its time. **He has also set eternity in the hearts of men.**" Just think of it. God has put into my heart (and yours) a sense of something greater than I which lives longer than my earthly life. There is a curiosity in each of us about what is yet to come. In most of us, that eventually translates into an understanding of a Creator who has made us and loves us. He has not "given me away" because He knew me before I was born and loves me.

Some of the adoptees have only recently learned of birth siblings and have been able to connect with them. The journey has started a healing process as well as bringing a sense of completion.

All these stories told started me thinking of heaven. Is this some of how it will be when we are joined again in heaven with others? Will the sense of family be a feeling of completeness? Will there be family members there that we never knew as family here on earth? The spiritual ties most certainly go far beyond our earthly families. I am just thinking about the possibilities of what we will know as "family" when we reach our final home.

Until then, let's enjoy and appreciate our families here on earth while we can. Remember, your brothers and sisters include far more than just the biological ties we know as siblings. We have a great family in this community known as White Station.

NOTHING LIKE SISTERS

Growing up, we were not all that close. Vera Jeanne is three years older and so much smarter. She and I were different in every way. Kathleen is five years younger. The difference between five years old and ten years old is a lifetime. The difference between 10 and 15 is childhood and teen years. You understand.

One year for Halloween, Vera Jeanne decided the three of us would dress alike and "Trick or Treat" together. That was a lot of fun because no one ever guessed who we were. I cannot remember how old we were that year, but I think I was in the fifth grade. Kathleen would have been in kindergarten. Vera Jeanne would have been in eighth grade. A wide spread. But I remember having a lot of fun together that night.

My next memory of the three of us girls doing anything together, just the three of us, was the summer of 1965. Vera Jeanne was living in New York. She was to be married in August to a Texan. She was moving back home (Colorado) for the summer until the wedding. After the wedding, she would move to Texas, where she has lived since.

Kathleen and I took a train from Chicago to New York City. Vera Jeanne met us at the train station, and we spent a month together getting VJ finished with obligations in New York. She then packed her little VW Bug with all her "stuff" and headed west. The trip was to be a couple of weeks with a stop in Philadelphia, DC, and Indiana for a few days visiting with grandparents and other relatives. Then we headed west through Oklahoma where I was dropped off to spend some time with my college roommate while VJ and K went on to Lubbock, Texas, where VJ was to see Steve, her fiancé, whom she had not seen in months.

While I was getting the worst sunburn in my life in western Oklahoma (my college roommate and I decided to get a beautiful, even suntan all over while we were harvesting potatoes—she lived out in the country so we stripped down to—well I won't even say), I understand the few days in Texas were very eventful. The joyful reunion, the cold feet, the calling off of the wedding, the begging to go on with it, K not knowing what to do, the negotiating of time with family—on and on. I am sure that story is remembered today very clearly three different ways.

Anyway, several days later, I caught a bus to someplace (I can't remember where) in Texas to meet up again with VJ and K to finish our final leg of the trip to Westminster, Colorado, which was home. I was sick from sun poisoning. VJ was a mixture of pre-wedding jitters, uncertainty, and many thoughts of making a horrible mistake. (BTW, she and Steve did get married and are still married these 50+ years later). Kathleen was a teenager who no longer had the idea of "marriage made in heaven, wedding bliss, the perfect match" or any of the things she might have been thinking a few days prior.

Fast-forward into our later adult years, the three of us sisters began to spend some time together every year. We have not lived near each other since VJ went off to college. So once a year, we would do something. Sometimes it was meet in Phoenix at K's house. One summer the time was spent in Jackson, Tennessee, with me at the Bed and Breakfast. They put in an herb garden for me. They arranged furniture and pictures. K stayed the entire summer setting up my reservation and accounting system, among many other helpful suggestions. (She also went home with her private pilot's license due to the eagerness of Glenn and K to spend concentrated time on flying lessons.)

The summer of 2007, the three of us met in Nashville where many of our extended family were gathering to celebrate the 50th anniversary of a cousin. It was that weekend that I suggested the three of us take a serious trip together. They each agreed and made a suggestion of a destination. My suggestion was a trip to Antarctica. With a little bit of bargaining and begging, the destination selected was Antarctica. That was the beginning of many months of planning. We set the date for early 2009. We cleared calendars and carved out three weeks for the trip.

I am not sure how much VJ and K knew, but this was the time that Glenn's early stage of Alzheimer's disease was beginning to manifest itself. Although he was diagnosed early and was taking medicine, it seemed that 2008 began to bring daily changes and signs that showed Glenn and me that our life was changing.

I cannot remember how much of these changes I shared with others. I am sure to some I shared too much. To others I might not have shared enough. I do remember it was a hard time for me. I was in denial many days. I tried to be the "perfect wife" with patience and understanding, filling in the gap, taking over all the financial and household duties and maintenance inside and outside.

Departure day for our trip finally came, and I was determined to enjoy the time. The three of us sisters met in Miami on January 29. We were off for a three-week adventure. It was wonderful! I was focused totally on the time with sisters and the adventure we had been planning for the past 18 months. It was perfect. Everything went great. Three weeks of a great adventure.

Then the last day in Santiago, Chili, while getting ready to make the trip to the airport to fly home, I received an email from Glenn which said he had lost a birthday card that I had prepared for him to mail while I was away. No big deal, right? It should not have been. However, it was the thing that reminded me what I was returning to. I had spent the last three weeks not thinking about the problem. For the past three weeks, I had not had to help him with daily activities, remind him of things, or cook for him. (He had insisted upon a very strict diet for diabetes which required constant preparation, weighing and measuring everything he put into his mouth, and preparing food for consumption five times a day.) The email was a reminder of what I had been able to forget for a short period of time.

By the time I joined VJ and K for a snack before leaving for the airport, I was crying uncontrollably. I don't know when I have ever done that. I could not get settled. We were in a public place, and I just kept on crying and trying to explain the joy I had had the past three weeks, not thinking about the circumstances I was facing. My reaction was far beyond reason. I knew it but could not stop. It embarrassed me and them, but it was a volcano of emotion coming from deep inside that had been building up for months and now came out.

Writing about it these eleven years later, tears still come up. That was a hard time! But my sisters were with me. They were patient. They listened. They did not try to stop me, did not tell me to get control, did not tell me things were going to be all right, did not once say "things are not as bad as they seem." They listened. They sympathized. They let me share and let me cry.

How did they know that is exactly what I needed? They are my sisters! That is how. I do not know what I would have done without them these past few years!

Since the trip in 2009, the three of us have made many wonderful trips together. It is just what I need each time. It is a break from the reality of living with an awful disease. I am so glad Glenn and I were able to continue to be together until July 2019, when Glenn was moved as a permanent resident of Job's Way, the memory-care wing here at Kirby Pines. It is a wonderful place, where each resident is cared for by very capable caregivers. I am able to walk to his place any time night or day to spend time with him. He seems content. Several times a week, he tells me he likes his place. He usually says, "We like this place, don't we." It is hard for him to understand why I am not with him at night. He thinks his room is "our apartment." But overall, he seems settled and happy with "our" living situation.

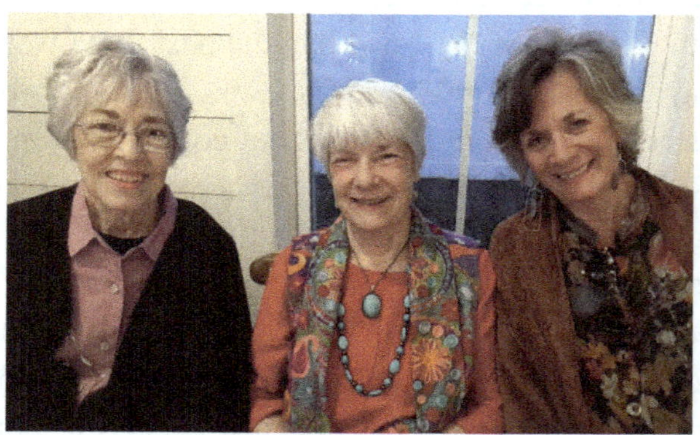

Three Sisters

*****

An addendum to this: Today as I am proofreading this, we are in the middle of the isolation created by the Covid-19 virus. Job's Way is now in "lock down" mode. I get to see Glenn via FaceTime, which is helpful. I did go around to the outside of the building last weekend. A caregiver in the facility wheeled Glenn to the window so we could see each other through the window. But that was even more frustrating than a visit via FaceTime. We could not hear each other. He could not understand why I would not come in. He became agitated, then we both were crying. I will not do that again!

"ADOPTED" GRANDCHILDREN

Once in a while, surprise relationships come along. Glenn and I found these relationships in the young children who belonged to the Hispanic family living next door to the Bed and Breakfast we owned in Jackson, Tennessee.

Glenn was working in the yard one hot summer day soon after we moved to Jackson. Two young boys, Jose, 5 years old, and Javier, 3 years old, came over to "help." They spoke no English other than "yes" and "no" and perhaps "Coke." However, children can make themselves understood. What they wanted was something to do and to have some attention from this man.

Glenn quickly found two large pairs of work gloves and two pieces of yard tools. I think one had a shovel and the other a rake. Both tools were far too large for boys so young to use effectively. But that did not matter. All Jose and Javier cared about was they were doing something and were getting attention from a man who did not seem to mind having them around.

This was the beginning of a relationship that has lasted all these years. An older sister, Jessica, later become a part of our family. Anna, the youngest sister, was born a few years later and is also a part of the group we lovingly call our "adopted grandchildren."

Through the years, Jessica, Jose, Javier, and Anna played a part in our lives. Since our blood grandchildren were geographically distant, these "substitute" grandchildren filled a place in our hearts that only time with a person can fill.

During these past five years, since Glenn and I have moved to Kirby Pines, these four children, now adults, have visited multiple times. They have given to us attention we have welcomed and sometimes needed. They send us reminders of our relationship by mailing mugs which say "Best Grandma Ever" and "Best Grandpa Ever." Although two live miles away in Indianapolis, they come for a quick weekend visit periodically. The two who live in West Tennessee, 120 miles away, make an effort to drop in for quick visits or call and check on us with a word of encouragement. All four have invited us to be a part of their lives and make sure we stay in touch. This relationship fills a very special place in our hearts. Three of these "grandchildren" have children of their own. Their children call us Great Grandma and Great Grandpa. We are truly grateful to these special people in our lives.

*****

A few days after writing the above memories, Jessica and I shared a nice TextMessage conversation. These pictures were a part of that conversation.

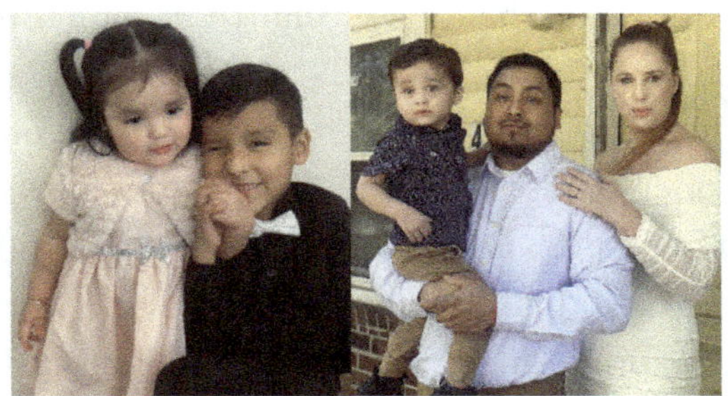

The Aguerra Children

LETTER TO JAVIER

Javier,

You have been such a special part of our lives since you first wandered into our yard next door to yours. At the time, you were only three years old, and you instantly won our hearts. You have been our "adopted" grandchild ever since. I believe you and Jose "worked" for Glenn about an hour that day, earning a quarter each, ensuring permanent work for us any time you have wanted it and needed it for the past 15 years.

Your favorite treat at our house after Wednesday night class and VBS sessions was a "banana slip with two cherries and no banana." (The cherries were never eaten, but they were a part of the presentation!)

You became a regular part of our lives, being our substitute grandchild, going to church with us through the years, taking airplane rides with Mr. Glenn, going with us on a family Christmas trip, beating everyone all week long in "SkipBo," and generally filling a big part of our lives and hearts.

For several years, you were our own private chef for Sunday dinner. Those were fun times with Anna setting the table, you cooking, and then spending the afternoons playing games. As you honed your cooking skills, you decided to prepare a formal meal at our house honoring Monda on her birthday in 2008. You prepared a four-course meal, set the table with the best we had, and prepared a wonderful meal with Monda's closest friends gathered to enjoy the evening of friendship and your beautifully prepared meal. That was a special time for all of us. Monda was so pleased, and Glenn and I were so proud of you.

Now you are about to graduate, have become a man, and are very independent. Your maturity has amazed us and pleased us. You have made us so proud.

You will always have a special place in our hearts and a place in our home any time you want or need it.

Love to you and best wishes to you as you carve your life out as an adult.

Glenn and Janice

Beyond Description

There are experiences that are beyond words. What are some of those in your life? Perhaps the beauty of a sunrise or sunset. The feeling of peace or power at the top of a mountain or beside a roaring ocean. The surprisingly over-whelming feeling when your first grandchild was placed in your arms. What is my point? I am trying to wrap my mind around the love of Christ described in Ephesians 3:17b-19:

*And I pray that you, being rooted and established in love,
may have power, together with all the saints, to grasp how
wide and long and high and deep is the love of Christ, and
to know this love that surpasses knowledge—that you may
be filled to the measure of all the fullness of God.*

The 1989 musical *Aspects of Love* is not remembered by most people. However, one song from the musical continues to be enjoyed by many:

Love Changes Everything
Love, Love changes everything:
Hands and faces, earth and sky,
Love changes everything:
How you live and how you die.

Yes, Love, Love changes everything:
Now I tremble at your name.
Nothing in the world will ever be the same.

Off into the world we go,
Planning futures, shaping years.
Love bursts in, and suddenly
All our wisdom disappears.

Love makes fools of everyone:
All the rules we make are broken.
Yes, Love, Love changes everyone.
Live or perish in its flame.
Love will never, never let you be the same.

(Lyrics by Charles Hart and Don Black, 1989)

Although these lyrics were written with human love in mind, in many ways they describe the love of Christ. Inspired by the Holy Spirit, Paul says this love "surpasses knowledge." We can continue striving to imitate Christ and to understand, in some limited way, how this love changes us. It does affect our actions and our lives. Let's be "rooted and established in love" while we live our lives following Christ.

A Glimpse of Heaven

This evening there was a group gathered in The Station of our Community Life Center for singing together. The room was filled with people of all walks of life. The ages ranged from an infant in a mother's arms to some near 90.

There were several song leaders. We sang and read scriptures in English and in Spanish. (Sometimes simultaneously and sometimes one language at a time.) Our skin and hair were different in color and texture. However, with all these differences, we were gathered with one purpose (to worship together) as one body (church at White Station).

The experience put questions into my mind about when we get to heaven. Will our ages be all different, or will there be one age? (Eternal?) Will there be many song leaders or one? (Perhaps an angel?) Will we be speaking in many languages or one? (Celestial?) Will our bodies be all shapes and sizes or one? (Heavenly?) Will we be all different colors or one? (Unflesh color?) Will we sing many songs or one? (The New Song mentioned in Revelation 5:9 and 14:3?)

These questions are interesting to ponder. We each will know the answers someday. But as for now, I am happy to enjoy the feeling that I have had one small glimpse of heaven this evening. I look forward to the next night of praise in The Station. And, yes, I look forward to the day when all the answers to the questions will be made known to me when we meet again on the other side of this life!

He Is the Joy

Christmas is nice
Holidays are fine
I always seem
To run out of time

The scurry of mice
The flurry of snow
The hurry of people
Wherever I go.

The trees are decorated
The presents are bought
The food is prepared.
Why am I so wrought?

The letters went out.
The cards are just fine.
My head is spinning.
I don't think I can dine!

What am I missing?
What is forgotten?
My soul is astir.
I feel so rotten!

What is it now?
What's my heart saying?
I need to take time
And begin praying!

Christ did come
Yes! A baby Boy
Now I remember.
He is the joy!

The Holidays: A Time of Loving and Sharing

The holiday season is in full swing. Here at White Station, the annual Holiday Ladies' Brunch traditionally marks the beginning of the holiday activities for our church family. Boxes for the fall food drive have been filled and returned. Much of the food has already been a blessing to families in our community. Turkeys have been donated to families. The annual Thanksgiving dinner prepared by White Station families and served to anyone who comes has taken place and was a blessing to all.

The red tubs for the annual Christmas party for the children in foster care are being filled with gifts carefully selected for a specific child with personal needs and wants. Plans for the party for these children and foster families are being made. Much effort goes into this event to ensure a wonderful time for all. College students in the Christian student center at U of M will be enjoying special gatherings. The Small Groups will share special events to celebrate the holiday season, taking this opportunity to express love and appreciation to each other.

Yes, "The Holidays" is a time of loving and sharing. It is a time to reflect on our blessings and to share with those not as fortunate. It is a time to be open to opportunities to enrich the lives of others. It seems to be full of creative and meaningful ways to bless and be blessed while sharing.

Just writing this and thinking of the activities that have already taken place and are soon to come, I get excited as well as **tired**! How about you? Maybe the best gift we could give to our families this year, and to ourselves, would be to simplify our own lives. What that looks like would be different for each person and family. The idea may not be appealing to some. But most of the people I know are trying to slow down a bit and have more quiet time rather than busy time.

The needlework piece shown on the front page of this issue of *Matters of the Heart* was lovingly created by a dear friend. Although this work took many hours to complete, the simplicity of the manger scene and visit from the shepherds and angel as shown in this piece is powerful. The God of Heaven, Creator of the universe, came as a baby, visited by shepherds and announced by angels, is an amazing story. Let's take time to think about this gift and the expression of God's love. When I think about it, I become calmer, happier, and more secure as I look toward a new year and toward my forever life. May you be blessed with a simple, powerful holiday season surrounded by love of friends, family, and God!

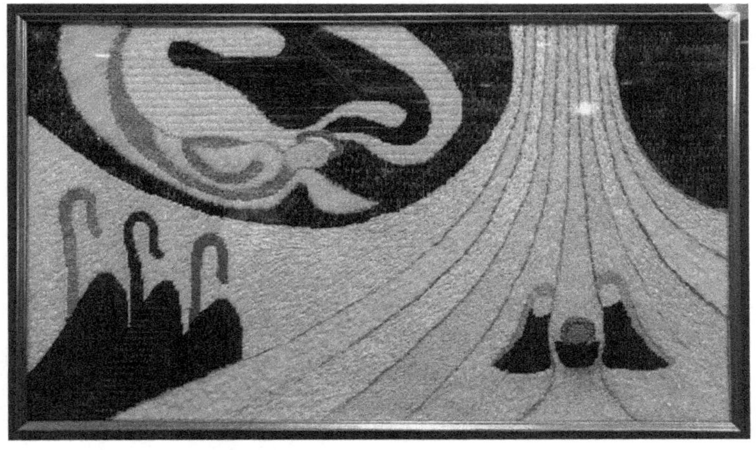

Needlework of Nativity Scene by Barbara Logan

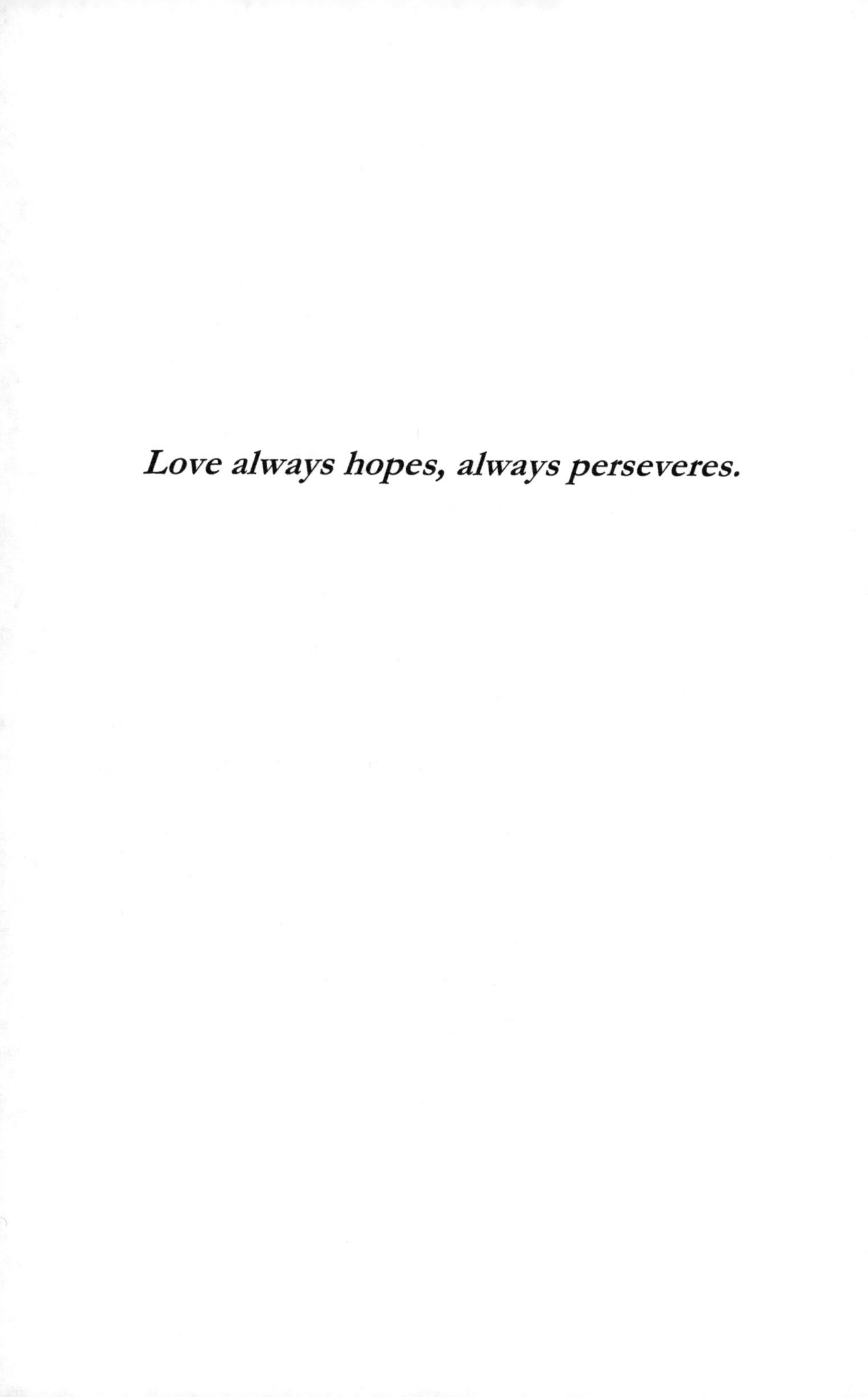

Love always hopes, always perseveres.

Welcome 2019!

Here we are again. At the beginning of a new year. New beginnings. New opportunities. A time to start afresh with those resolutions, goals, challenges that we so diligently make for ourselves.

Looking back, my personal list two years ago was:

* Start each day with prayer, study, and meditation.
* Treat others with respect and kindness.
* Control my tongue.
* Be patient.
* Lose 10 lbs.

Worthy goals. After two years, they are still "goals." However, just the conscious effort to work on these things has made me, perhaps, a person who is more pleasant to be around. Maybe I am more like the person I want to be and God wants me to be.

So, I ask again, how are you doing with your annual list, your "resolutions"? Is it worth the process? If so, let's begin again with making a list and putting forth the effort to keep those commitments. (I still have those same 10 lbs. They stay on my list—and on me—year after year. Right now I have only 15 lbs. to go!)

A new year has begun. New songs to be sung.
We turn a new page as we continue to age.
We can face this new year with others so dear.
At White Station we know as a group we can go
Into these new days like walking a maze.

Our SAM team along because we belong
To a wonderful bunch who will (is my hunch)
Be right there beside me when I ache in my knee
And back and my feet. Some will give me their seat
When they see that look we can read like a book.

We are at that age when we turn a new page,
We open our eyes and readily surmise
That life is great fun when we go as if one.
We can make it just fine to the finishing line!

The Dot-to-Dot of Our Lives

Recently, Rodney's sermon used a dot-to-dot puzzle to effectively illustrate that it takes the talents of each member of our fellowship to complete the picture. This morning, it occurred to me that each of us has a "dot-to-dot" puzzle for life. It is so interesting to look back over the events and years, thinking about how this picture has come together.

During the last semester of college, my "job-search plan" was to sign the first contract offered. (This shows how free-spirited—immature—I was.) That "plan" seemed to work out very well. For the duration of my working life, my maturity level must have stayed the same. The "plan" did not change throughout my working career.

Reviewing the events which have brought me to this current place in life, it amazes me how each personal and career step along the way has led to the next phase of life, which has been just right. The dots have been connecting, and the picture is nearing completion.

Aging certainly has its benefits. It is so much easier to clearly see God's hand in life. My "mature" way of looking at it is that God has a "dot-to-dot" outline for each of us to work through. The Holy Spirit helps guide us along the way. We have the choice of following the plan or taking our own path.

When we take a different path, God will lovingly urge us back on track. He will help us make a beautiful picture if we let Him guide us. Or we can continue to go our own way and make a mess of it. We have choices. God has made a plan.

Something Beautiful

Something beautiful, something good;
All my confusion He understood.
All I had to offer Him was brokenness and strife,
But He made something beautiful of my life.

(Lyrics by Bill Gaither, 1971)

How is your dot-to-dot picture coming along? Are you happy with the way it is looking? God is still helping you fill in the blanks. Rodney pointed out that someone else needed to fill in the spaces with color. Maybe that is what God is doing. He is not finished yet. The end result will be something beautiful!

"Happiness Is Overrated." Really?

"Doc Martin" fans immediately recognize this bit of wisdom. Doc Martin, the TV character, believes and lives it.

One of the many beauties of living into these "golden years" is that we do see life through different circumstances with added experiences behind us. Don't you have a totally different perspective now than when you were younger? Thankfully!

Not many years ago, when I first became acquainted with Doc Martin and heard him state the bit of wisdom, "Happiness Is Overrated," it struck me as funny. It just added to the grumpy Doc Martin character portrayed so well. However, "Happiness Is Overrated" is beginning to make more sense to me.

Thinking back over your life, when are the times you would say you were the "happiest"? Was it when you got your driver's license, that great passage to adulthood? Perhaps it was when you were named Homecoming King or Queen or whatever seemed important at the time? As years accumulated and life moved on, what made you "happy"? Marriage, the birth of a child, or the biggest of all, grandchildren?

Right after marriage, I remember feeling "happier" than ever before in life. The sense of peace, joy, and security brought about "happiness." However, experience teaches all of us that not one stage in life remains the same. Change is the very essence of living a life.

What is high on your list of *Important, Must Have,* or *Absolutes* for life? If a survey were taken of people at our stage in life, my guess of the results would be: Peace, Joy, Security, Love.

Those are the ingredients in the recipe for happiness. Each comes from living a life of faith. That life of faith comes from being in the word and trusting God. Optional ingredients in that recipe might be: Good Health, Strength, Comfort. Of course, there is always the big one that most of us would add: A Good Night's Rest!

Nowhere does the Bible promise "Happiness" at all times. Perhaps Doc Martin is correct. Happiness is over-rated! But trusting God for peace, joy, security, and love is not overrated.

MOVING DAY: THE KIDS

As you can imagine, the day Glenn was moved to Job's Way (memory-care wing) was a very emotional day for the entire family. I don't know how I would have handled it without the kids. Cindy, Glenna, and Raymond were here to do the actual physical move and to give emotional support to each other.

The staff members in Job's Way were very helpful. At our family meeting, the head nurse for the medical areas and the nurse in charge for the floor were both there to address all our questions and concerns. They explained many procedures and issues we should anticipate without our knowing to ask. They were kind, supportive, and understood the tears.

The kids took everything they thought would help Glenn feel at home in his new living area. They were able to reproduce Glenn's office walls by transferring every family picture and special bits of memorabilia which had been around his work area and desk in the apartment. Instead of Glenn's desk, he now had his LazyBoy in the new space. The recliner was the one item Glenn always mentioned from the first day he and I spoke about the impending move.

The time with the family meeting and the moving of items and the arranging and decorating the walls and shadow box outside the door took most of the day. It was a long, tiring day. But the kids were there to do the job. What a blessing that was!

WALKNG THE JOURNEY:
LEARNING FROM OTHERS*

The path of this journey we are walking is filled with others walking along before us, next to us, and behind us. When we are in a place of joy, we can look around and enjoy the company of those who are also rejoicing. When we are in a troubling place, there are also those who are experiencing these times along with us.

The ones I am watching carefully are those who are a few steps before me. They are helping me find my way. They are showing me faith in the promises of God being with me. There are friends who seem to be just months ahead of me in the journey. Those are the ones to whom I am looking and from whom I am taking my cues and following in their wake.

It is such a comfort to have friends who have deep faith who are swimming the troubled waters, climbing the highest mountains, walking through the dark wilderness. They are my beacon of light, my guideposts, my light at the end of the tunnel.

Perhaps you have been asking yourself "Why am I HERE?" Part of that answer may be to encourage others in this journey. You may be HERE to help me in such a time as this!

Thank you, dear friends!

*Written August, 2019 as a special "Thank you" to my dear friend, Sydney Wagner.

"Teach Me Thy Way, O Lord"

Teach me Thy way, O Lord, teach me Thy way!
Thy guiding grace afford, teach me Thy way!
Help me to walk aright, more by faith, less by sight;
Lead me with heav'nly light, teach me Thy way!

When I am sad at heart, teach me Thy way!
When earthly joys depart, teach me Thy way!
In hours of loneliness, in times of dire distress,
In failure or success, teach me Thy way!

When doubts and fears arise, teach me Thy way!
When storms o'erspread the skies, teach me Thy way!
Shine through the cloud and rain,
through sorrow, toil and pain;
Make Thou my pathway plain, teach me Thy way!

Long as my life shall last, teach me Thy way!
Where'er my lot be cast, teach me Thy way!
Until the race is run, until the journey's done,
Until the crown is won, teach me Thy way!

(Lyrics by Benjamin Mansell Ramsey, 1919)

Several months ago, Leon led the song "Teach Me Thy Way, O Lord." As we sang this song together, I became a child again in that small congregation where my early years were spent.

What a powerful thing music can be. For those of us who were blessed to grow up in a church community, worship music holds a special place in our hearts and memories.

For me, those memories are wonderful. They are full of the love of many adults who were a part of my "rearing," although they were not a part of my biological family. My friends and first "puppy loves" came from that group of people. The social life of our family revolved around that group in a small building literally built by those men and women.

Some of the "new" praise and worship songs are equally as powerful to me. "In Christ Alone" brings tears to my eyes every time we sing it. "I Can Only Imagine" moves me in a way that I cannot put into words. There are many on my list which I enjoy in a group setting and in my own home during my alone time.

But there is just something special and powerful about those songs we sang in that small congregation, surrounded by the people who were a major part of my life during those formative years. They bring a smile to my face and a peace to my heart.

A Word about My Friend, Marilyn Cobb Sanderson
by Janice Petty Wall

As editor of *Matters of the Heart* since July 2015, my goal has been to offer encouraging thoughts without drawing attention to myself. Though many of the stories and emotions have come from personal experiences, I have tried to make them applicable to most anyone in our Senior Adult Ministry. The only time a "Written by" credit was given was when someone other than myself wrote the article.

However, unique circumstances perhaps allow unique writing. Thus it is that I am sharing some very personal thoughts as we experience a "Changing of the Guard" here at White Station.

Leon Sanderson's 40 years of service have been celebrated and acknowledged and very correctly done. He has touched the lives of almost everyone and anyone who has passed through the doors here. He has helped us grow up and has seen us mature as a family of God's people.

Now, I would like to share a word about my friend, Marilyn Cobb Sanderson. Please humor me while I make these heartfelt, personal observations.

Marilyn and I met on Labor Day weekend of 1966. She had just turned 22 years old a few days earlier. I had turned 22 three weeks earlier. She came from Harding College (via Springfield, Missouri). I came from Oklahoma Christian College (via Denver, Colorado). We first met in a diner on the south shore of Long Island. Three single women were "interviewing" me as a possible roommate. (Being poor school teachers, they needed a fourth person to share living expenses in a four-bedroom Cape Cod house.) Apparently I passed the test; they invited me to join them.

Little did Marilyn and I realize at the time that this was the beginning of a friendship that has lasted all these years. We have shared years of careers, travel, church families, and personal families. (Our husbands, Leon and Glenn, are brothers-in-law.)

Marilyn is, and has always been, one of the most spiritually mature people I know. In all phases of her life, she has truly followed Christ. Family and friendships are dear to Marilyn. In all the years since meeting her, I have never known her to hold a grudge toward or speak of a dislike for anyone. She never speaks ill of anyone.

Sunday was wonderful! Seeing all the family and friends who gathered to wish Leon and Marilyn well warmed the hearts of all who gathered. So many came from the Memphis area. A large number came from miles away. Some of the friendships represented recent acquaintances. Many represented almost a lifetime. Some of our members cannot remember a time when Leon and Marilyn were not a part of their lives, either through Harding Academy years or growing up in the church family of White Station.

Leon and Marilyn, your presence among us is going to be greatly missed. There will be those who step up to the plate and will fill the void. However, you two will be remembered and loved for all you have done for White Station and for all you mean to us personally. "Retirement" does not mean the end of friendships. It does mean a major "Changing of the Guard." Know that you are loved by all.

Love never fails.

Final Traffic Pattern

The east/west traffic pattern for the Memphis International Airport goes over the building where I live. As I enjoy my morning coffee on the balcony, the airplanes flying in are just overhead. The approach can be heard from a distance out. Then the sound is just above my top-floor apartment. If there is a cloud cover, sometimes I can feel vibrations as they pass. I can hear this sound every morning and every evening. However, the pattern is just enough south that, no matter how far I dare stretch over my north-facing railing, I cannot actually see the planes. The roof over the balcony blocks the view.

Some might think this sound is a nuisance. But I don't. As a retiree of FedEx, it is a sound of security. It is the sound of many hours of work. It is the sound of my retirement still being available. It is the sound of a large portion of my life before retirement. As an avid traveler in my younger years, it is the sound of that final leg of the journey. It is the sound of returning home after seeing a new part of the world or visiting with family and loved ones. It was always a good feeling to land safely home!

This morning as I was enjoying the freshly washed sky left by the storm of yesterday and all seemed especially right with the world, I began to think of the presence of God in my life. Just like the planes, I know He is there. I hear the sounds, and see the signs, and even feel the "vibrations" in so many ways. However, I do not see Him. My physical home blocks the view of His face.

Someday my physical home will be left behind and nothing will block the view of that eternal home and the face of God. All will be visible then. The storms of today will be over, and I will be able to see clearly.

I imagine that someday all of us will say, "Oh, it is so clear. Why couldn't I see this before?" But until then, look for the signs, listen for the sounds, feel the "vibrations." Everything is pointing to the final traffic pattern. Follow the path, and continue with faith that you will land safely home.

VISITED BY ANGELS UNAWARE

During these last few years of Glenn's rapidly declining health and my increased concerns, we have been visited by angels unaware. The angels' visits in the Bible are spoken of in this way. It was Abraham—sometimes others—who was unaware that the visitors were angels. In our situation, I am sure the visitors had no idea how much of the angel role they were playing at the time.

It seems so appropriate to send a huge THANK YOU to those of you who took the time to come a long distance, to make the effort to "drop in," during these times. Some of you might have sensed how critical these visits were. Some of you probably had no idea how much the visit, your time, and effort meant to me.

Nieces and nephews from my side of the family have come from Texas. Denise and Jason came and played mah-jong. (They had the nerve to win!) Glenn laughed the weekend Alexander came and spent two nights. It amazed me how Glenn connected with him. Glenn laughed more that weekend than I have seen him again. Janice Kay and Chris stopped in with their wonderful children. It was so good to see them and have a quick visit.

Of course, the occasional visits from my sisters and sister-in-law have all been very timely and supportive. They didn't have to take the time to come for a visit. But they did. Time with each of them has been precious.

Betty and Marie, Glenn's sister and her daughter, have visited. Oh how Glenn loved that! Again, that weekend, Glenn laughed with them. They told and retold stories. They jogged memories that were precious. These visits seemed to bring a peace to Glenn that nothing else could have brought. It was the right visit at the exact time when it was needed! It is a long, hard drive from Montgomery, Alabama, but it was better than any medicine Glenn could have taken. Thanks!

Those of you who visited are greatly appreciated!

WHAT DO YOU SEE?

"What you see depends on where you stand." Have you ever heard that? Have you thought about that? For example, before a person has a child, they can see exactly how a child should be disciplined. However, when that person is standing on the other side of the "child" issue—after their first is born—that view often changes! Then when they stand as a part of the parent of a second child, that view is refocused again.

Where do you stand in life? What were your priorities when life was great and you were young and healthy? Now that you have traveled down some bumpy roads, and even maybe some detours along the way, what priorities have changed? Has life become refocused?

When you were standing just after that first love, marriage, and great health, how did your life of the future look? Now that you stand after the marriage is down the road, perhaps has been very rocky, maybe even coming to a screeching halt, is the view of marriage different? Have your priorities been refocused?

What did you see before the financial breakdown, the loss of a job, or the loss of your house? Are your views of God, values, and priorities more in focus now? "Do not worry about your life, what you will eat or drink; or about your body, what you will wear. Is not life more than food, and the body more than clothes? Look at the birds of the air; they do not sow or reap or store away in barns, and yet your heavenly Father feeds them" (Mt 6:25-26). Do these words have more meaning and comfort now than before?

How focused are you now that you have heard some ugly words in your life: cancer, death of a loved one, drug addition, rejection, Alzheimer's disease...? Before you stood in a place where these words existed in your life, did you view eternity differently? Does this new place of standing help you focus more clearly on God and His love, peace, and hope? Has standing in the "Shadow of His wings" become more dear to you?

Walking through the "Valley of the Shadow of Death" has a way of giving us a new vista. We can see life from an entirely new viewpoint. This can be the beauty of our journey. "What you see depends on where you stand." Is the view better today than it was forty years ago? Or is it just different from when you were younger? If we stay focused on our Father, things should become clearer, more easily understood, and much more hopeful **because** of the bumps and the detours—not **in spite** of the difficulties.

What do you see?

Rejoice in the Lord always. I will say it again: Rejoice!
Let your gentleness be evident to all. The Lord is near.
Do not be anxious about anything, but in every situa-
tion, by prayer and petition, with thanksgiving, present
your requests to God. And the peace of God, which
transcends all understanding, will guard your hearts
and your minds in Christ Jesus (Phil 4:4-7).

You, Lord, are my lamp;
the Lord turns my darkness into light (2 Sam 22:29).

You turn my wailing into dancing;
you removed my sackcloth and clothed me with joy,
that my heart may sing your praises and not be silent.
Lord my God, I will praise you forever (Ps 30:11-12).

Never will I leave you;
never will I forsake you (Heb 13:5).

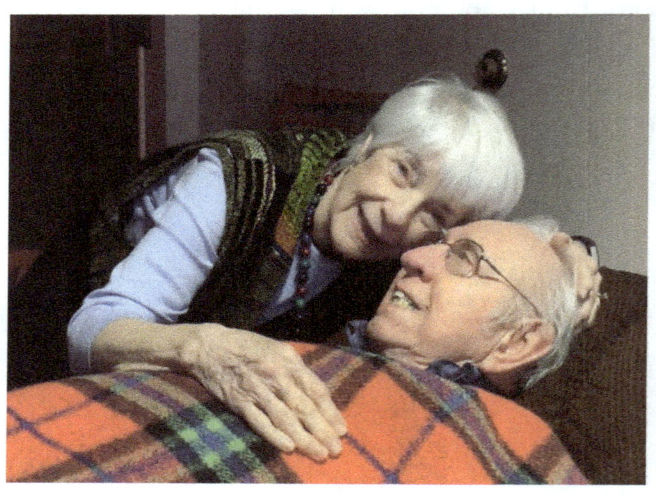

Janice and Glenn Wall on Moving Day

A PLACE TO CALL HOME

What would I be doing if Glenn and I had not moved to Kirby Pines? I cannot even begin to imagine. The help we have received through this journey the last three years has been amazing. Each step of the way, Chris Palmer has been alongside to counsel us, support us, and help with understanding the stages and what is coming next. When the time came for Glenn to phase into the Day Care services in Job's Way, the step was easily made. After several months in Day Care, a space became available and Chris was right there with needed information and encouragement.

Glenn has now been in his new "home" nine months. He often says, "I like this place." Sometimes he states, "We like living here, don't we?" The nursing staff has been great. The CNAs have a way of connecting with every resident, each playing a special part in making this new living arrangement, the place we call home, just what Glenn needs. They make it a place I know is just what we both need.

There is no way I can name all the special team members who serve Glenn so well. However, I would like to especially thank Iris and Shapell, extraordinary nurses; Patricia, who takes special care of Glenn on the evening/night shift; and wonderful Elizabeth Sweet and Brian Odhiambo, who make it possible for Glenn and me to have a few minutes of FaceTime during these unusual days.

Each of you has a special place in my heart. There are no words to express what you mean to me and Glenn, meeting special needs we could not do ourselves.

THANK YOU!

ONE FINAL PERSONAL THOUGHT

It is now April 21, 2020, and time for me to wrap this "Journey" up. We are several weeks into the "Stay at Home" restrictions and social distancing. You can easily remember these days. Hopefully, we all will think about ways we actually benefited from these days. Today is one of those days I will think about with thankfulness and joy. Please indulge me while I share one more personal story.

One of the greatest losses for me with Glenn living in Job's Way, not having the "old" Glenn with me, is his continuous encouragement and support. He believed in my ability to achieve goals, encouraging me to try things I might not have tried. (Example: The last two positions at FedEx were my favorite of all jobs. I would not have pursued them without Glenn convincing me to "go for it.") Beyond this, he was a great supporter during illnesses.

January 2020, a recurrence of lymphoma was found in my body. These "sneaky little cells," as the oncologist calls them, were found first in 1997. A round of radiation sent them scampering. They showed up again in 2015. Glenn was far more concerned about them than I and the oncologist were. It touched me so much the evening we got the call that lymphoma was found. Glenn was so concerned. He held my hand and promised he would be by my side the entire time through whatever treatments would be pursued. Assuming we were facing chemo therapy, he said, "I will be there to hold your head as you are vomiting." Now I ask you, isn't that the sweetest, most supportive thing you can ever hear from a husband?

So this time, when the "sneaky little things" were not so sneaky, or so little, Glenn was in Job's Way. Knowing this would be something for Glenn to worry about and not be able to do a thing about, I have chosen not to share the news with him. The ones with whom I have shared are my sisters, my WWTCHMA friends (Marilyn and Sally), the mahjong group, and the Wednesday night group. (Each of these have been the subjects of "Thank you" articles in my "Journey of Loss and Encouragement.")

Today, when I returned home from the last of 20 radiation treatments, I was welcomed by a beautiful site. There was a spread of healthy food, gifts, cards, and a vase of flowers. The ladies of the mahjong group and the Wednesday evening "girls" have been my local encouragement and support during these four weeks of painful sleepless nights and daily trips to the clinic. Today, they gave me the gift of love in this beautiful expression of care, concern, and shared joy for completion of treatments. What better way is there to surround a friend with love?

Thank you, dear friends, all of you mentioned in this book! Life is impossible without friends. You have given the encouragement needed to press on.

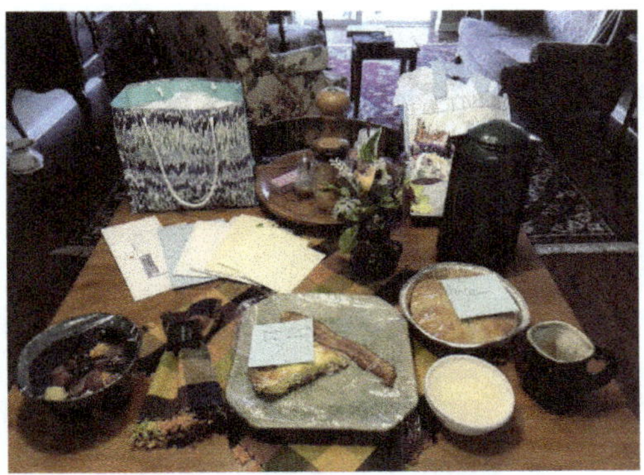

The Gift of Love

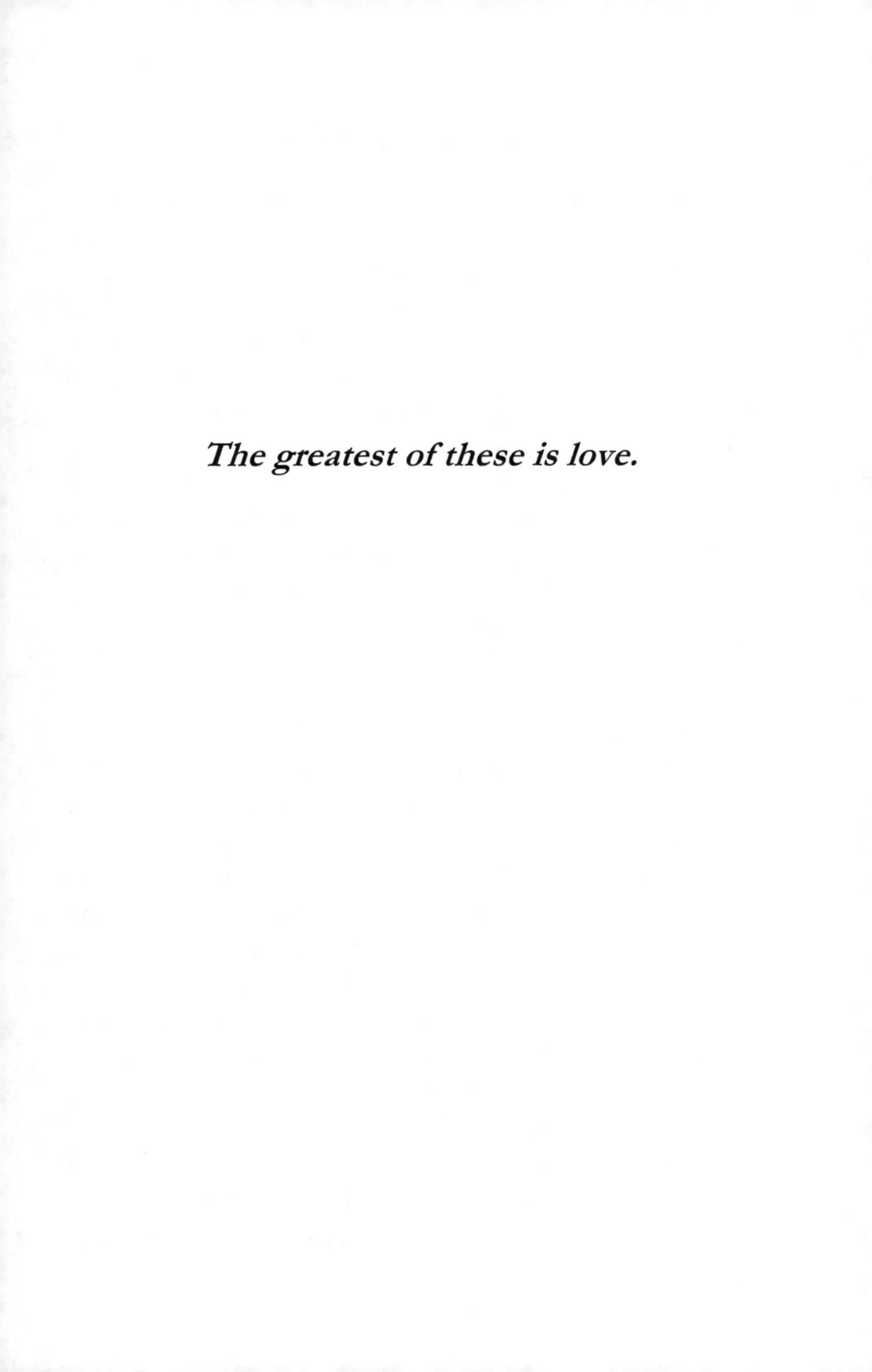

The greatest of these is love.

ACKNOWLEDGMENTS

Some projects sit in a mind for a few months before taking shape. *Matters of the Heart: A Journey of Loss and Encouragement* has been in my mind several months, forming as each day passed. I knew it was critical to express to others how much difference their acts of kindness have meant to my sanity and life. However, being a person who has difficulty expressing my deepest feelings, I had no idea how to find the way.

Often during those times, I found myself unable to sleep. During those times, I would sit at the computer and pour my thoughts out through my fingertips onto the screen. Some of those thoughts and feelings have found their way into this book you are now holding in your hands.

Jean and Andy Saunders moved into Kirby Pines Retirement Community, therefore into my "neighborhood," months ago. Although I have known Jean many years, we had not been more than speaking acquaintances. Jean is the reason this book is completed. It has been a joy to work with her.

Since the first mention of this project to Jean, she has worked magic. Jean took on the challenge of organizing material, editing writings, polishing the work, and encouraging it along the way. She has the knowledge that is required to bring a book from "vision" to "done." Jean had contact with Paul and Catherine Wilcoxson and their printing company. She has the skills required to get a project not only completed, but completed well.

Thank you Jean, for the enthusiasm, energy, skill, and patience this project has required. Thank you for understanding how important this tool for saying "thank you" has been to me. For your gentle ways of correcting my work, guiding my thoughts, and keeping me engaged, Thank You!

And, of course, to each of you who is mentioned in this book, another huge "thank you" goes your way for being by my side and a part of my life during these years. It is my hope that you have an idea of how much your time, love, and care have meant to me, even though it might not have been expressed sufficiently to you.

I love and appreciate each of you,
Janice